THE PHOTOGRAPHER'S PRICING SYSTEM

Get paid what you're worth for portraits and weddings

ALICIA CAINE

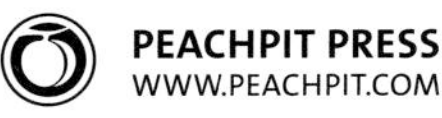

PEACHPIT PRESS
WWW.PEACHPIT.COM

The Photographer's Pricing System:
Get paid what you're worth for portraits and weddings

Alicia Caine

Peachpit Press
www.peachpit.com

To report errors, please send a note to errata@peachpit.com
Peachpit Press is a division of Pearson Education.

Project Editor: Valerie Witte
Production Editor: Danielle Foster
Development and Copy Editor: Linda Laflamme
Proofreader: Kim Wimpsett
Composition: Danielle Foster
Indexer: Valerie Haynes Perry
Cover Image: Shutterstock.com; Copyright: Stocked House Studio
Cover Design: Aren Straiger
Interior Design: Mimi Heft

ISBN-13: 978-0-134-18167-7
ISBN-10: 0-134-18167-0

9 8 7 6 5 4 3 2 1
Printed and bound in the United States of America

To the Profit First Photography community—my people.
You're an epic glitter bomb of glory.

ACKNOWLEDGMENTS

My heart is overflowing with gratitude to be given the honor of sharing my experience and knowledge. My hope is that it gives even just one of you a life-changing experience in your business that begins a ripple effect with others.

First of all, Gordon, my husband and champion. I'd be still working at McDonald's if it wasn't for you. Thank you for trusting me with every single insane idea and letting me be more of myself. I love you forever and always. My children, Jordon, Trinity, Joshua, Alessandra, Caleb, Bradley, and ThaliaGrace. I can't believe that I get to be a mommy to such incredible souls. You fill my heart with so much joy.

My personal assistant, Kim Rodgers. The best of best friends who sees me better than I see myself, has seen me at my worst, and continues to stand beside me. Your enthusiasm for everything I do never ceases to humble me. Thank you for just being you.

My Profit First Photography team, Angela Lindley, Natalie Gowen, and Suzanne Haverkorn. I am honored to call you friends. I hate the miles that is between us all and can't wait to have my island someday so we can all live on it together.

Kresta and Daniel Morgan, for giving our little family hope when we were feeling at our lowest and welcoming us into your life and home. You truly are the most epic of friends.

To the wonderful Peachpit Press team that shared their talents and gifts with me to birth this baby of mine: Danielle Foster, Kim Wimpsett, Aren Straiger, and Mimi Heft.

Valerie Witte, my project editor. Thank you for being patient with me and my inability to ever figure out the whole FTP thing. You made this experience an incredible one for me and a dream come true. Linda Laflamme, bless you for sticking with me and my wonky grammar and often ridiculous use of punctuation.

Christ, may you be glorified through this work.

And last of all, to *you* readers. Thank you for trusting me, allowing me to share my heart and my experience with you. Thank you for giving me the opportunity to serve you. My business is built around the hopes and dreams that I have for you, and it never ceases to delight me when I get the opportunity to be a part of your epic stories.

CONTENTS

INTRODUCTION

Confession: I'm not an amazing photographer. I'm not naturally creative with my art, and I am better at duplicating technical skills than I am at creating original pieces of photographic art. I'm not known in "those" circles as a rockstar photographer. I spend more time on my iPhone camera than I do with my Canon Mark III.

My heart has always been for business. My first camera (a Canon 20D) was a way for me to document my life and family, but that camera brought me to the point of being a business strategist for nontraditional photographers. It was a means that I pursued and that led me to my true passion: teaching what I learned the hard way so others don't have to go through the fog of figuring out how to make a business out of photography.

Let me explain. In 2007 with very few camera skills and even less business experience, I made the wildly audacious decision to start a business of photographing babies and children in natural light. At the beginning of the year, I was getting $200 sales, and by the end of the year I was getting $1600. By the end of my second year, I had my own natural-light studio space and was averaging $8000 per client with a high-sales, low-volume business model. So how did I go from $200 to $8000 sales in just two years?

By constant refinement of my pricing! I refused to commit to pricing that wasn't giving me the results that I needed. Instead of studying business books on pricing, I studied my clients. I began to test ideas on them and get their feedback on what they wanted and what they weren't willing to pay for. Then I calculated a dollar amount that I knew my business needed to produce to be able to be profitable and sustainable. Pricing became a process of commonsense thinking mixed with strategy and a crazy spirit of persistence and tenacity.

After being sought out by other photographers, sharing my pricing system with them, and seeing them get the same results in their business, I knew I was onto something: a simple system that has evolved into the book you now hold in your hands.

How this book can help

But, *The Photographer's Pricing System* is so much more than just a book on how to create pricing. It is about pricing for your perfect client and ensuring long-term profitability and sustainability for your business. Here's a chapter-by-chapter breakdown of what you can expect:

- **Chapter 1**, "Getting Started," covers all the juicy details that every other pricing plan ignores and that form a crucial foundation without which even a perfect pricing menu would crumble. I fully believe that a business can be built with your head in the clouds (big thinking) while having your feet firmly planted on the ground. Chapter 1 is where you ground yourself. When you look at your situation realistically for what it truly is, you'll better find answers and solutions to the things that weren't connecting or were failing to work.
- **Chapter 2**, "The Ideal Client and Your Marketplace," builds on your foundation to reinforce the profitability and sustainability of your business. You'll learn how marketing and pricing go hand in hand, as well as the importance of research to identify your ideal client—that person who not only values you and your art but is willing to pay your price to have you serve his or her needs.
- **Chapter 3**, "Reverse Engineering Your Pricing," is where you crunch the numbers for your collections, prints, albums, and specialty items. All the prep work you did laying a foundation in earlier chapters will make this process easy. This chapter is also the one that you will keep coming back to each time you (and your business) are ready for growth.
- **Chapter 4**, "The Grand Reveal," brings it all together, showing you how to populate your collections and debut your new pricing to the world. It's real, baby.
- **Chapter 5**, "Pricing Consistency for Weddings and Other Specialty Sessions," has got you covered on how to tailor your pricing for wedding and mini-session work, ensuring those offerings remain consistent with your brand and that you maintain the same level of profitability in all that you do.
- **Chapter 6**, "Troubleshooting Guide," answers common questions, smoothing those bumps along the way to profitability and sustainability that we all encounter. I've also included an extensive resources section for your further learning pleasure to take your experience to the next level beyond this book.

- **Expert's Guide**, "Market Less, Get Paid More with a Niche That Fits," shows you how to transform yourself from an ordinary photographer to an expert who specializes in a niche subject. Everyone knows experts get paid more, and they also draw clients like magnets. This bonus guide shows you how you can too.
- **Worksheets** appear throughout the book to help you tally numbers, survey clients, refine your signature workflow, and more. This is your book—go ahead and write in it! Practice what you're learning by filling in those worksheets. If you prefer to keep your book neat and tidy or you want copies so you can revise your thoughts and numbers as your business grows, you can find the same worksheets online.

  To download the worksheets and the gross-earning calculator, set up an account at peachpit.com. Enter the book's ISBN or go directly to the book's product page to register. Once on the book's page, click the Register Your Product link. The book will show up in your list of registered products along with a link to the book's bonus content. Click the link to access the files. Download them when you're ready to work or log on and start downloading now so you can be ready to go—just make sure you remember where you put them.

Remember, there are dozens of ways that you can price yourself, and they all have their merits of why they work. There is no one way to sell your photography. What is most important is that what you do is profitable and sustainable and it feels good to your soul. If you don't believe in your pricing, no one will.

Create the time to try

For you to be successful with the pricing strategies in this book, you must make this process of researching, number crunching, and implementation a priority. Your brain will love to assure you that you'll get around to the task when you have the time. But the truth is, if something is not immediately a priority, it generally won't become one down the road when the sense of urgency wears off. Right now, you feel the urgency to tackle your pricing, which is why you purchased this book. You know you need this right away. Make sure that it doesn't get pushed away.

I am a firm believer in scheduling education and time to implement. If it isn't written down, it isn't real. The best intentions rarely follow through. Reading each chapter and working through its worksheets will probably take you two to three hours to complete apiece. No biggie, right?

Right now, I want you to go to your calendar and schedule three one-hour blocks of time on three separate days to go through each chapter; be sure to leave a day to digest in between sessions. For example, read through a chapter in Monday's one-hour sitting. Digest for a day on Tuesday. Come back to the book again Wednesday, and spend an hour re-reading the same chapter and going through all its worksheets. Digest for Thursday, and return to the chapter on Friday for a final hour of refining and tweaking the worksheets.

You will never become financially free if you don't get serious about your pricing. Not only will investing in your business help you achieve better profitability now, but it will also help you build in sustainability so that you have a business that will be thriving for years to come.

Replace fear with hope

The mind is a beast sometimes. Even if we make learning everything that we need a priority, the fear of the unknown still can take over, disabling us from moving forward. All the "what if" questions and worst-case scenarios start pouring in. What if no one ever hires me? What if I kill my business because I jumped too fast too high?

Guess what. Sometimes the worst-case scenarios happen. But usually, so do the best-case ones as well.

Being an entrepreneur, you are never guaranteed that your actions will produce absolutely amazing results only. When you work for yourself, you are taking a greater than normal risk to earn a livelihood. You never know where your next client will come from—ever. Even the mega-million companies don't. Being in business for yourself will be a series of failures and then success. Sometimes it will feel like more failures than wins.

When you embrace that knowledge, you can be able to face those nagging fears and questions because you are willing to accept that the risk is worth facing the fear. The *best-case* scenarios will happen only if you step into the risky place. Instead of focusing on the worst-case scenarios, focus on the best-case ones. If you don't see any hope, what will be the motivation for taking the next step? You can do this.

Be patient with the process

Nurturing a fledgling business can be overwhelming. You need to focus on a million and one things—your client workflow, marketing, managing your website, blogging, bookkeeping, customer service, editing, management, and administration—all at once, or so it seems. We usually convince ourselves that we are just going to fail because we don't know everything right away, and we see our business as lacking *so much*. Knowing everything, however, isn't as important as implementing a few things well. So, be patient with yourself and be patient with the process. Only soak up as much information as you can immediately implement effectively.

It's a process that will involve a lot of trial and error. You're going to go through hard stuff, and you're going to make mistakes. That's normal. None of us can completely prevent it, because every time you obsess with anxiety over one aspect of your business, something that you never could have anticipated hits you from a different area. It happens to every successful business owner out there, so it's a waste of energy and brain capacity to focus on all the things that you are afraid of failing in.

When your mental wheels are constantly spinning, you'll find that you really aren't being all that productive. You'll find yourself backpedaling instead of moving forward. I want you to give yourself permission to accept that not everything is going to get done perfectly or even just get done. It will be okay. Just focus on what you can do now. Set a timer if it helps. Do your best. And then accept that you aren't going to get it all done and not everything is going to be done perfectly. Sometimes your business will be like a plane that you are building while you are flying it. Most businesses are doing that very thing. No one has it all together, and no one is getting everything done. There is no reason to beat yourself up for expectations that are completely impossible to satisfy. Be gentle on yourself, and just focus on one thing at a time.

One of the things you will learn through this experience and reading this book is that growing a business is an exercise in constant refinement, one that you should try to go through consistently. Settling into what you love to do and just staying in that comfort zone is easy but not ideal. Sustainability requires evolution. Rival photographers will always be working hard to evolve in their businesses. If you stay settled where you are, you run the risk of losing clients because your competition is now excelling in areas where you once might have dominated.

Being in business is a constant battle presenting new challenges all the time. If you start finding that you don't have challenges and things are getting easy, be on your guard. You could be neglecting something or becoming complacent. Contentment and complacency can look very similar.

Build on a solid foundation

Your passion for what you create is not enough to build a solid foundation in your business. It's not enough to make you profitable, even if you are a phenomenal photographer. Your business will succeed only if it is built on a successful foundation.

Pricing is only one of the building blocks in that foundation, as you'll learn in later chapters. I've worked with hundreds of photographers who created their pricing and came back to me to say that it completely failed and they needed help creating a new price list. There was nothing wrong with the price list; their business foundation was weak, and their focus was not on what produced the most profitable results for the effort.

If your prices aren't working, you can keep lowering your prices and lowering your prices to find that sweet spot where you get hired without having to market, but you soon will have to come to grips with the reality that you just lowered yourself into a hole that digging out of will be painful or nearly impossible. It's much easier to fight growing and moving forward if you start taking steps backward just to get by. Don't fall into this trap. The sections that follow offer some lessons I've learned that underpin all the advice to come in the rest of the book. I know it's tempting to skip ahead, but resist the urge. You wouldn't skimp on your house's foundation, so why risk it for your business?

Imperfect action is better than none

Running a business is not an intellectual exercise, it's a performance exercise. It's more about the doing than anything else. Action is always required, even if you can only do it imperfectly.

So, how can you start to take imperfect action?

First, you need to actually go into your calendar and block off time in your day to work on your business. Decide right now where you are going to dedicate time to do this and mark it in your daily calendar. Write down the *day* and the *time* that you will be working on your business and do not devalue that time by distractions by web-surfing and bouncing around on Facebook or letting the phone keep interrupting.

If you put it in your calendar and treat it like a business appointment, you know that your time is devoted to that activity and you won't fill it in with anything else because it now has a high priority. That way, your whole day isn't lost spinning around inside your business doing management and administrative tasks. You'll be amazed how such a simple step can make such a huge difference.

If you find yourself unable to follow through with the scheduled tasks, it's probably because you are being hit with some internal resistance. If you find yourself focusing on things of lesser importance, like playing with new Adobe Photoshop actions, searching for new album templates, or designing new wall galleries, it's possible that you are avoiding and hiding from getting out there and doing what you know you need to be done. It's okay if you find yourself there; it happens to everyone. But you need to bring awareness to why you are doing what you are doing so that you can confront those fears and inner resistance, understand what is going on, and handle it.

If you find yourself in that place, take notes, journal, and process your feelings about what is going on.

- Are you afraid of taking on new responsibility?
- Does it feel like being forced to grow up and you're not ready?
- Are you afraid to fail?
- Are you afraid of being successful?
- Are you afraid that you are not capable?

As long as you are an entrepreneur and taking risks, you are constantly going to be dealing with fears. They don't go away; they are necessary emotions that trigger our fight factor. If we never feel urgency, we become passive, and we lose the will to take the next step. Being aware of those fears and identifying the resistance is what is going to keep you moving forward because you won't allow yourself to settle into the fear and own it.

Just remember, procrastination is always a part of the natural process, but when you break down what you do into small and manageable steps, facing your fears and tackling your tasks head on, you'll start to make progress and success will come. Don't beat yourself up, forgive yourself for giving into the procrastination, and get back on the horse and ride.

Manage your time

You're meeting your tasks head on, but what if their sheer volume is pushing you under? Here are a few time management tips and tricks to make sure you get the most out of this book because you had the time to dedicate to it:

- Work during the times you are the most productive.
- Schedule important tasks, such as appointments. If it isn't written down, it's not going to happen.
- Delegate the distractions. Ask for help with the laundry! (You aren't going to get help until you ask for it.)
- Take breaks. The body and mind need a day of rest. Make sure you schedule downtime, and stretch often.
- Eliminate time wasters. Or at least, limit the amount of time you devote to them. If Facebook isn't adding value to your life right now, for example, don't be afraid to go on a hiatus for a month. Look for things that don't add value to your life and find ways to reduce, eliminate, or delegate.
- Let go of what doesn't matter. Not everything is going to get done.
- Work on only one thing at a time. Multitasking is not productive.
- Celebrate what you accomplish. You did it. Even if it was imperfect, it was better than not doing it. Throw many dance parties along the way!
- Have fun through the process!

Resist the next big idea

When you are in the initial stages of business and in growth mode, you will find yourself at times convinced that you have to keep coming up with new ideas to be able to get big results. But the truth is, business growth is about bringing in more money. Mathematically there are three straightforward ways to do this with the business you already have; you don't have to add weddings, babies, children, seniors, business headshots, food photography, and an Etsy store selling landscapes just to bring in more money. You don't need to add more to what you are doing; you need to narrow down and perfect one or maybe two things and refine your business. (You'll learn more about this in the Expert's Guide.)

In the beginning phases of your business it is better to refine what you currently are doing than to keep adding to the list of the thing that you are capable of doing to be more profitable. The three most important areas that you need to be focusing right now are

- **Increasing your number of clients or customers**: This is where marketing comes into play. For your business to grow, you need to promote what you do and why you are the best choice. Your focus needs to be on your visibility, not just on what services you can provide. Do not fall into the trap of spending more energy planning mini-sessions than marketing them.
- **Increasing the amount of money you earn per transaction**: The profit-first system focuses on bringing in more money with each transaction. You can take a slow track or a fast track, but either way you choose, increasing the amount you are making per transaction is a step closer to having a business that thrives and sustains itself.
- **Increasing the amount of repurchasing and return clients**: Marketing to your past clients with customer service and follow-up marketing. Your relationship with clients should not stop once they have their orders delivered. You know they already love you and they value you; continue marketing to them so that they can continue seeing a need for coming back to you.

These are the three most important areas that you need to be focusing on at all times in your business to ensure and maintain profitability and growth. I know it sometimes feels like you need to step up your skills with photography in posing, lighting, and editing. But those things don't bring in more clients, they don't bring in more money per transaction, and they also don't guarantee returning clients. The skills will come with time, but the business requires them to not be of the utmost importance to be able to profit and sustain itself.

Ask for feedback or help

The most successful business ideas out there rarely are created in a vacuum. You need a people in your life to bounce business ideas off of. Surround yourself with like-minded people who are pursuing similar goals as yours to keep you motivated and help you refine your ideas—but don't give up your complete decision-making power to anyone.

Just for you, I created a Facebook community of like-minded people who all have the goals and desires to be profitable in their businesses. Join the community here: www.facebook.com/groups/thephotographerspricingsystem. Bounce ideas off of them at any time, and seek out their support.

Always keep in mind that not everyone is perfect, just like you aren't. Be gracious, be authentic, and treat others like you would like to be treated. When you come together in a spirit of teamwork and all helping each other to raise the bar together, you will build a community that is inspirational as well as prolific.

Don't get discouraged

All the business success stories I have read of famous entrepreneurs talk about their constant uphill battles. This is what happens when you take on the battle of being responsible for your own livelihood. If you are uncomfortable with fighting and dealing with curveballs, being in business for yourself is going to quickly bring you to a point where you have to make a choice: Face all your greatest fears, or succumb to failure because you gave up the desire to fight. You only succeed as far as your greatest fear. If your greatest fear is that you will be rejected for your pricing, that's as far as you are going to go.

You will never be the best-priced photographer; there will always be someone cheaper or someone giving better value. There will always be someone who has a better studio, better packaging, a better website, a better blog, and all those things. There will always be someone who you can use as a measuring tool to determine what you can and can't do. Either you can accept those limitations as determining factors on why you can't move forward or you can be the best person who serves your clients in a way that no one else does. You can focus on the things that make you amazing, or you can focus on the things that everyone else does that are better than what you do. One way or the other, what you choose to do is what will determine the outcome of your business—not the economy and not the oversaturation in the industry. It's what you do with all of those elements and how you choose to rise above them that will help you succeed. Believe in what you are doing and the purpose that it serves.

If your business is only for side money, that motivation to keep fighting is not going to be strong enough to get you through incredibly hard times when clients dry up and your marketing efforts don't seem to be working at all. Those times will happen. If you struggle with feeling you're not worth your prices, even after you know what it will take to build a business to sustain itself, then I encourage you to spend some introspective time trying to pinpoint what really, truly is the source of those feelings of doubt and unworthiness. Money is just an exchange system of what you value for what someone else values. My hard work for your hard work. When life is over, how much you have or don't have matters little compared to what you did with it.

So as you go through this process of creating and then debuting your new pricing, I encourage you to give it your very best. And remember, whether you think you can do this or you can't, you'll be right. This is just a step, and there are many more steps to come. Enjoy the process that each one brings you because it is a gift that you have to be able to take your passion and turn it into profit. Celebrate each sale as a gift.

1 GETTING STARTED

When setting goals for your business, it's important that you know exactly how much you need to make, exactly how much you want to make, and *why* you want to make that amount.

It's tempting to just skip this step and let the cards fall where they may. You can wish, hope, and pray that the money you need will come when you need it or that you get fixed a specific amount—but without a good understanding as to why you need that amount, your prayers may not be answered. When there is not a clear motivation for needing your business to produce a certain amount, the urgency to make that goal turn into a reality simply is not there.

Even without a fact-based reason for needing to achieve certain financial goals, you may still feel the pressure that you should be producing something. But when you can't break down exactly how much you need to make, you won't be able to produce a plan of action for exactly what you need to be doing in your business to be making sure that you reach those goals.

That's why it is incredibly important that you go through this exercise. Please do not brush over it. It's not going to be tons of fun, but I promise that the numbers are going to be revealing. They'll help you give up any misconceptions and assumptions that you currently have about your business's profitability.

Setting realistic financial goals

Financial goals are incredibly important—but there is also a fine line between optimism and delusion. For a new boutique photographer to set a goal to be making $300,000 in his first year of business is completely delusional if he has nothing in place to accomplish those goals. To mentally intend does nothing.

Before we get started on pricing and how we are going to actually achieve your goals, let's take a step back. First we have to get clear on what your goals really are—and *why*.

As I said, this is going to take a little work. But fret not, it's not going to be intensive. This is not a perfect method—it's just a starting point for those of you who are in desperate need of clarity.

tip Putting yourself in debt to start a business is setting yourself up on the hardest road you can take to owning and running a successful business. This may be the only alternative you have. So, understand what you are investing in and that it will demand more of you in terms of what you need to produce—and that the start-up investment needs to be paid back.

To start you off, in a nutshell, here's my personal philosophy about being in business and the ideal way to handle the money and expectations of what the business needs to produce: For a business to be considered profitable, you can consider only the money that is coming in *after* all investments have been paid back *and* after the expenses.

Here's how starting a business works: It all begins with a start-up investment from personal finances or a loan. If you borrow money from your personal finances, that should be paid back just as if you were borrowing money from a bank.

You are probably rolling your eyes that I felt I had to explain that. But most people I work with do not understand that a business is not in a healthy place until the start-up investment has been replaced. While some may say you never need to pay back the personal finances from your business, make it your intention to do so and to approach your business with a professional and profitable "business owner" mind-set.

The important numbers: budget and expenses

The following is a worksheet for numbers you need to go and dig up right now. This exercise will give you more realistic goals, even if there are some missing elements. You can always tweak and adjust later—we just need a starting point for you to work with.

BUDGET & EXPENSES WORKSHEET

Monthly/yearly overhead expenses: ______________________________

(includes Internet, phone, Photoshop, cloud storage, electricity, gas for your car, accountant, email service, office supplies, etc.)

Business debt: ______________________________

(how much have you borrowed—that you need to pay back—for all start-up costs, including camera, computer, equipment, etc.)

Monthly/yearly marketing budget: ______________________________

Monthly/yearly educational budget: ______________________________

Business savings account: ______________________________

(how much you currently have set aside)

Savings for equipment: ______________________________

(how much you currently have set aside)

Monthly/yearly personal income: ______________________________

Desired monthly/yearly income: ______________________________

note Income is not how much your business brings in from session fees and sales but how much you pay yourself after all business expenses and taxes. Income = paycheck.

You can lump together your expenses for a year or for a month. Go with whichever sits best with your brain for easy number crunching. We'll be referring to these numbers more in the future, so have them nearby for easy reference.

Assessing your work time

This is a tricky one that most entrepreneurs struggle with: understanding how much time they actually have to work.

There is no such thing as a part-time business. There is only full time. While you may not be spending 40 hours a week on the clock doing business tasks, there is still a demand that will *mentally* require 40+ hours of you. If you want a part-time job, starting a business is the worst way to achieve that. It just is unrealistic to expect a 40-hour-a-week income out of a business in the start-up years when you are investing fewer than 20 hours into its growth. And growth requires a lot more than just dealing with clients.

You can agree or disagree with me, but my opinion is that you should be spending no fewer than 10 hours a week focused solely on marketing and education geared toward growth. Start planning for that now so that you can always have the time to implement what needs to take place in your business to grow and to ensure you have the time to improve your business skills.

So while you are planning the next year and setting goals for profitability, take a calendar and start scheduling time for your business. Do it now, ahead of time, so that when you plan ahead for the next six months, you are always spending Tuesdays and Thursdays on your business marketing and growth. And don't schedule other things on top of the business appointments you make with yourself!

When you honor your business as a *business*, the people in your life will honor it—as will your clients. If you don't honor your business hours, don't expect anyone else to do so.

Just to start off, follow these basic steps:

1. Looking at your calendar for the next 12 months, block off any time that you know you won't be available to work—for example, you have previous commitments, there are holidays that you want to take off, and so on.
2. Decide how many days per week you'd like to dedicate to your business.
3. Determine how many hours per day, and which hours, you are going to establish as your business hours.

(NOT) WORKING FROM HOME

Working from your home is both a blessing and a curse. There is amazing freedom that can let you blow that Popsicle stand during a high-stress time and take the kids out for fro-yo in the middle of the day on impulse. But there is also a downside because it's easy to slip into complacency and just allow your business to be treated like a hobby and not dedicate and honor the hours that it needs for growth and sustainability. Take responsibility for the time you invest in your business—which may mean finding a way to commit to actually working in the home office, not doing laundry, cleaning out the refrigerator, going to yoga, and so on.

To work through Chapters 1 and 2 of this book, you are going to need to know how many:

- Weeks per year you will be working in the next 12 months
- Days per week you will be dedicating to your business
- Hours per day you will be dedicating to your business

tip For consistency, ease of scheduling, and keeping boundaries, I suggest having specific days—if not hours of the day—that you dedicate to your business. Being too flexible can make your life too hectic.

How much time do you really have?

Is the number of hours you want to invest in your business even possible? Or do you have even more time that you are currently spending on something of lesser importance? For example, five hours a week of housecleaning could be outsourced for $15 an hour, allowing you to spend five extra hours per week taking on an extra client—and earning more money (**Figure 1.1**).

To get an idea of how much time you really have for your business, go through this weekly calendar and block off time slots for the following:

- Personal time (exercise, reading, talking on the phone, spending time with friends, etc.)
- Family time (dedicated time for family, kids, and/or spouse)
- Activities (work, religion, sports, family, etc.)
- Client hours (shooting, sales, phone calls, etc.)
- Business and admin hours (editing, blogging, writing, email, marketing, office work, etc.)
- Education and growth (online training courses, workshops, seminars, books, personal coaching, etc.)
- Appointments

tip If it helps you categorize your time better, use colored pens so that you can see exactly what counts as business, personal, and household time.

	MONDAY	TUESDAY	WEDNESDAY	THURSDAY	FRIDAY	SATURDAY	SUNDAY
TIME							
5:00 AM							
5:30 AM							
6:00 AM							
6:30 AM							
7:00 AM							
7:30 AM							
8:00 AM							
8:30 AM							
9:00 AM							
9:30 AM							
10:00 AM							
10:30 AM							
11:00 AM							
11:30 AM							
12:00 PM							
12:30 PM							
01:00 PM							
01:30 PM							
02:00 PM							
02:30 PM							
03:00 PM							
03:30 PM							
04:00 PM							
04:30 PM							
05:00 PM							
05:30 PM							
06:00 PM							
06:30 PM							
07:00 PM							
07:30 PM							
08:00 PM							
08:30 PM							
09:00 PM							
09:30 PM							
10:00 PM							
10:30 PM							
11:00 PM							
11:30 PM							
12:00 AM							

Figure 1.1 My week at a glance

After you have a visual understanding of what an average week looks like, ask yourself the following questions:

- How many hours per week, on average, can you dedicate to your business?
- How many hours per week do you realistically need to dedicate to your business—is there more than you currently have?
- How are you able to give your business more hours? (What must be sacrificed?)
- How can you protect your household/family time to keep business and extra activities from taking over?

Where you are—and where you want to be

No matter where you are in your business right now, this chapter is going to be the foundation that you will always come back to when you reassess your goals and your pricing.

Almost everyone starting out in business downplays the importance of pricing and how it determines the direction of your business and its overall profitability. It should be the most important thing that you focus on in your business. In fact, it should be determined before you even begin to consider starting your business.

Yep. That's my stance. And here's why.

Is it going to be worth it?

Let's say you knew exactly how much money you needed to make a profit, how many hours you could invest, and how many clients you could take before you even started your business. If those numbers didn't add to being worth your while, would you still move forward?

Logic would say, "Heck, no! Why would I move forward doing something that makes no sense?" But reality says, "Oh gosh, that's exactly what I have been doing. I actually have no clue if I can even make a profit at what I'm doing and yet I'm still moving forward."

Isn't it wiser to crunch the numbers beforehand and plan all that out to see whether the investment of time, money, and effort is worthwhile?

YOUR HOURLY VALUE

We all know that time is valuable. But when you're a business owner who's not on the clock, you're probably completely clueless about exactly what your time is worth in dollars, right? Let's try to work it out.

Let's say you need to make $50,000 in gross sales annually, you want to take off six weeks every year, and you have an average of 20 hours per week you can give to your business.

Here's the math. First, calculate your weekly gross income (before taxes):

Desired annual gross sales (pretax): $50,000

Weeks worked per year: 46

Weekly gross sales* = $50,000/46 = $1087 per week

*(Gross annual income divided by weeks per year)

Next, calculate your hourly income:

Weekly gross sales (pretax): $1087

Hours worked per week: 20

Hourly gross = $1,087/20 = $55 per hour

*(Gross weekly sales divided by hours per week)

In this example, your hourly value is $55 per hour.

note Keep in mind that these calculations are to give you a rough idea of how much money you need to be making per hour to achieve your desired gross sales. These calculations do not work the same when billing clients your hourly rate. In Chapter 3, "Reverse Engineering Your Pricing," I will explain how to use your hourly value to create pricing for your hourly rates.

Now, following the previous example, calculate what your time is currently worth.

Desired annual gross income (pretax): $ ______________________

Weeks worked per year: ______________

Weekly income = $ __________________

Next, calculate your hourly income/value:

Weekly income (pretax): $ _____________

Hours worked per week: ______________

Hourly income = $____________ per hour

I've worked with several photographers for whom we did all the number crunching to realize that the business wasn't worth it to them. And guess what? They were relieved. After spending some money on coaching, they knew that the numbers weren't going to add up for them to be satisfied—and I just saved them a lot of heartache and financial loss.

Maybe you are in that place where you get clarity that it just isn't going to be worth the effort. Or maybe you are in the place where you see what the business is going to require of you to meet your goals, and it gives you hope and clear focus because you know exactly where you are going to have to invest your time and energy to make that happen.

That's why pricing is so important. If you can't make your pricing work just in number crunching, it's most definitely not going to work with your clients either.

The problem with poor pricing

The problem with most photographers' pricing is that they pick numbers they feel comfortable with or slightly uncomfortable. And most forget the crucial element of reverse engineering their pricing to see whether it's even possible to earn an income with those numbers.

And that is the reason why we have an oversaturated marketplace. If most understood that they would have to bring in $100,000 in sales to get a $25,000 paycheck, probably most would look to get hired just as a photographer's assistant or second shooter and walk away with that as a paycheck without the responsibility of management, marketing, administration, and everything else that comes along with the business-owning territory.

But there is this desire to have the freedom of time and flexibility, to be the one to make the decisions, and to feel satisfaction from creating something—and having someone else pay for that.

There are so many amazing benefits to being in business for oneself that if you are willing to fight the misconceptions and delusions and to get completely clear about what is involved and what is required, go for it. There is nothing more satisfying than being in business for oneself and creating a life by your own design. Sure, being an entrepreneur is emotionally challenging—but it's also emotionally satisfying. Most would choose to make $25,000 working for themselves over making $25,000 working for someone else. For me, even when times are incredibly tough, I know that I would never have the same satisfaction if I were working for someone else, even if I were making more. That's because it's not about just money; for me it goes deeper, as I'm sure it does for you.

It's not pricing alone that makes you profitable

To build pricing that is sustainable and profitable, you have to price yourself where you need to be, not where you currently are. And for a business to be sustainable, it has to be able to provide for the things that secure the future and not just be focused on what pays for the now. It also has to give you the most bang for your buck: Every hour counts. So, let's touch on two essential profitability factors: development and time management.

Growing yourself is growing your business

Profitability cannot be reduced to just a price list. It's a plan for the future, and then you create the price list to implement that plan. Most pricing systems are focused on overhead, taxes, and cost of goods. But rarely are outsourcing, marketing, savings, and education factored into the budget.

When you start thinking about pricing and profitability, you need to know what areas of your business you need to be investing more time and energy in. Learning social media? Learning how to write better blog posts? Networking? Marketing? Financial management? Website copywriting? These are things that are invaluable for a business owner to know because they all produce more clients—and more clients means more sales.

Time is money—and outsourcing yields both

Profitability is also in how you are managing your time. When you know your hourly value—which is what we're covering in this chapter—you'll find that you may be doing tasks that are killing your profitability.

Let's say you have 20 hours per week to focus on your business, and you need two clients per week. Generally you spend ten hours per client: six of those hours are in editing, two in shooting, and two in sales. You have nothing left for time to focus on marketing or making more money—your 20 hours of work per week are maxed out.

And let's say your hourly value is $50 an hour. That means those six hours of editing are worth $300 for each client, or $600 for both clients. But! You could *outsource* the culling and editing, which costs you $100 at $50 per session—and now you have 12 hours freed up! You can spend those 12 hours on taking in another client session, which will easily pay back that $100 in culling and editing, or use those 12 hours for marketing and business growth.

So, would you rather save $100 and not be able to focus on your business and its growth? Or would you rather spend the $100 to free up 12 hours and laser-focus those 12 hours on marketing and development?

INVESTING IN YOURSELF FOR NOW AND FOR THE FUTURE

There are endless business resources for you and a zillion things to learn and implement. You will never run out, not for a lifetime. But remember, these are investments in the future—they don't all pay off immediately. You have to learn before you can implement, and sometimes the implementation process can take a while before it gives you a return on your investment. For example, most marketing efforts can take months or years to bear fruit.

That's why it's important to have several things going at once, including things that will pay off now and in the longer term. That is sustainable thinking: What do I need to know for my present marketing effort (like social media), and what do I need to know for my future (like copywriting, networking, email-list building, and blogging)?

OUTSOURCING: SPENDING MORE TO PROFIT MORE

Every time you feel like you don't have time for something, assess where you spend the most time that you could possibly free up by outsourcing tasks to others. Then use that time strategically to invest in the things that bring profit and growth.

For some, housekeeping is an amazing place to start. You can find a housekeeper for as little as $15 an hour. If you have someone come in for 10 hours a week, that $150 can provide you with the time to take on an entire session that may bring you in $1000 or more. Wouldn't that trade-off be worth it?

These are things that you will be focusing on from here on out: what can you outsource so that you can focus on building growth and making more money?

That is sustainability. It looks to what will give the most bang for the buck. These kinds of things—business development, time management, and outsourcing—are going to be mental shifts that you will need to be constantly making in your business to ensure profitability.

Profits aren't determined by experience

One of the biggest misconceptions that photographers struggle with is that their experience should determine how profitable they are allowed to be. That is simply one of the most false assumptions one can make about being in business. There are few businesses out there that charge based on experience.

Generally, when companies increase prices, it has to do with either demand for their product or service, improvements in quality, increase in cost of goods, or inflation. Rarely does anyone charge for having more experience in their field of work. Even a doctor can't command more after 20 years just because she has put in 20 years—unless the quality of those 20 years are in alignment with that experience.

If every business raised their prices every year because they have another year of experience under their belt, a business would be completely unaffordable if it lasted more than 20 years. Plus, they would also have to find new markets every year because their target market would no longer be able to afford them.

What *should* determine your pricing

There are tons of factors that go into determining price, no matter what product is being created and what the company's end goal is. This fact is true for every industry out there, from cars to clothes to restaurants to doctors.

Photography is no different, which is why you can't just swipe someone else's price list and make it your own. You are not going to share the cost of goods and operating expenses, and you aren't going to be sharing the same goals, marketing efforts, and educational experiences. You may even not be striving to appeal to the same market.

For example, there are tons of car manufacturers out there producing vehicles in the $25,000 to $50,000 range. There are fewer in the $100,000 to $250,000 range, and even fewer in the $1 million to $2 million range. But the thing is, even if the demand is the greatest in the $25,000 to $50,000 range, it doesn't stop the $1-million-car manufacturers from making their product. They know who their customers are, and they know they are getting into that marketplace to take on fewer clients overall—and they price themselves accordingly. The $1 million car has factored in every element beyond just cost of goods, from design to marketing to customer service.

The same is true for photography. Don't be intimidated to price yourself such that you can provide what you know your business needs and your clients want. There is a client for every price point out there.

So, unless you are doing exactly the same things that other businesses are doing—from how much you are investing in your marketing to the quality of your products to your education budget to your overhead—their pricing, even if it works for them, is not guaranteed to produce profitability and sustainability for you, even if it does get you sales.

But sales is not the goal we need to focus on. Profitability and sustainability are.

Charge your clients not where you are but where you need to be

My local salon's stylists have three tiers of pricing based on experience. But even though my stylist is the middle tier, she is only higher priced because she has been in business longer and has more of a reputation and trust factor than the newer stylist. Thus, she can charge more because there is more demand for her services. Her clients know her better—they all book her by name.

Meanwhile, the lower-tier stylist usually takes people in from off the street—she gets all the newcomers. It has nothing to do with the quality of her work; it's just the demand for her services is lower. When she finally has a few years under her belt, a solid returning client base, and additional training, then she'll be able to raise her prices. It's a process. You aren't going to see the master stylist charge $500 for a cut and color, the middle-tier stylist charge $150, and the lowest-tier stylist $25.

A lot of photographers feel that when they start out in business, they have to offer rock-bottom prices and earn their way to the top as their experience grows. They feel they need to start out at less than $250 before they can even consider charging $1500 or $5000—even though they have the overhead and earning needs that require them to do so.

This is, quite simply, both untrue and not okay. Actually, it makes the journey to the top longer and harder because it can hurt your business reputation with word-of-mouth marketing when your prices start out super low and see constant increases.

MORE RATE HIKES, FEWER CLIENTS

With each significant pricing increase that you make, you are going to lose 75% to 100% of your current clients. It's incredibly difficult to raise prices and still keep the people who love you. So when considering a price hike, bear in mind that while you may keep a few loyals, generally you will lose the largest bulk of your clients.

If you are going to invest in marketing efforts, you really want those efforts not to be just for new clients but for repeat clients who will keep coming back to you year after year. It's easier to keep clients and get them to come back than it is to market and attract new clients who you'll serve only once.

To be able to secure your repeat clients, you need your prices to be where you aren't going to keep losing them. If you are doing increases of just 10 percent, your loyal customers probably aren't going to notice these slight changes and refinements. But if you are doubling your prices, you are going to lose them.

This is why I encourage you to start out with prices where you need them to be, not where you think you are.

If you are trying to be on a fast track toward building your business, having negative chatter going around that you are constantly raising your rates is not going to do well for the sustainability of your business. People aren't going to get super comfortable with you because they will just assume that even though your current prices are working for them, more than likely the next time they need images you are going to be out of their budget. That's when customers don't even consider emotionally attaching to you and making you their go-to photographer.

I know that I had to contend with that in my first year of business. I had so many people say wonderful things about me and then end it up with "but then she raised her prices." That's not the note you want people to be left on. Raising your prices is necessary, but if you can avoid as many increases as possible, the better it will be for maintaining the client base that you want to have returning to you, as well as the longevity of the word-of-mouth marketing they provide. I lost tons of clients that first year in business because of price increases—not a single client returned from my first to second year. That was a lot of lost marketing effort. I had to work extra hard the second year to keep bringing in new clients because I wasn't getting any returning customers.

And remember, if you want to build a business on sustainability, it's easier to market to people who already have given you money and love you than it is to constantly be focusing your marketing efforts on bringing in new people.

So, that's a huge reason why you need to price yourself where you need to be. The marketing efforts will be significantly easier once they are in place, and your profitability will be greater because you aren't investing as much time and money into marketing efforts.

Thinking—and charging—like an entrepreneur

If you have business growth that needs to take place, the money for that growth has to come from somewhere. Where is it going to come from? Your clients! They are the ones who are going to pay for your marketing, for your education (including this book!), and for your computer and camera. Your clients don't just pay you for your time and cost of goods. They pay for every aspect of your business. And when you build a price list that is focused on covering just taxes, your time, and cost of goods, you will be forever reliant on your second income—or main family income—to keep your photography business alive.

When it requires a second income to keep a business alive, it is delusional to think that the business is going to be a healthy, sustainable one. If your business is in the red and it takes a second income to keep it running, then you are wasting your time. And not only are you hurting yourself, but you are also hurting the person who is working their butt off so that you can throw money into a black hole.

I want you to be completely honest with yourself while you go through this book. One moment of truth is this: If you have been in the place where your business is not profiting, you must be willing to shift your mind-set from business-delusional to business-professional. You aren't just a creative photographer anymore; you are a professional entrepreneur.

Embracing being an entrepreneur doesn't mean you are going to have it all together. You will have to learn everything, just like all other entrepreneurs do. While business may come naturally to some, it doesn't come naturally to everyone. Now that I have been going at it for a while, it's become more natural to me, but it doesn't mean that every area of my business just clicks. I still have areas that I'm trying to wrap my head around, like Pinterest and Google ads.

I know, as a budding entrepreneur, there is a lot to learn and a lot to do. My advice: Don't be intimidated by what is ahead of you—it's not going to come rushing at you all at once. You can't do everything, and it's okay! Just focus on doing one thing at a time, implement it, and then move on to something else. You should always, always, *always* be in a place where you are learning something new, implementing, learning something new, implementing. Launching a successful business and becoming a savvy entrepreneur is a journey and a step-by-step process; it's not a single experience that's going to just happen and then poof! You just get it. Give yourself time and patience to learn as you go—and grow.

(Mis)handling gross earnings

note To work through this section and the calculator, download the gross-earning calculator Excel document, available with the rest of the book's worksheets and extras, by registering for the book at www.peachpit.com.

Okay, let's get down to numbers.

The first thing that I am going to walk you through is the gross-earning calculator (**Figure 1.2**). Just to make sure you understand the meaning of gross, it is the amount you make before there are any deductions. So it includes all your session fees, sales payments...every dollar that comes into your business.

PROFIT *first* PHOTOGRAPHY™
GROSS EARNING CALCULATOR

$42,000 Fill in desired personal income goal	**How much do you want to earn in personal income?**		

Healthy Budget

$50,400	Taxes (IRS, bookkeeper, CPA)	30%	
$42,000	Paycheck	25%	
$25,200	Cost of goods sold (COGS)	15%	
$16,800	Overhead	10%	
$8,400	Marketing (ads, direct mail, etc.)	5%	
$8,400	Saving for emergency funds	5%	
$8,400	Education and growth	5%	
$8,400	Outsourcing	5%	
$168,000	**Revenue (sales)**	**100%**	**Annual business gross earnings (sales & session fee)**

Start-Up Budget

$42,000	Taxes (IRS, bookkeeper, CPA)	30%	
$42,000	Paycheck	30%	
$21,000	Cost of goods sold (COGS)	15%	
$21,000	Overhead	15%	
$4,200	Marketing (ads, direct mail, etc.)	3%	
$7,000	Savings for emergency funds	5%	
$2,800	Business education and growth	2%	
$140,000	**Revenue (sales)**	**100%**	**Annual business gross earnings (sales & session fee)**

Figure 1.2 Gross-earning calculator

Before we get down to brass tacks, I'm going to let you in on a little secret: You have to gross a lot to make a living. A big shocker that every business owner will discover when it comes to profitability and being able to pay themselves—which is why we do this, right?—is how much has to be made to earn a personal income.

I have seen a few extreme ways of handling gross earnings, which are quite dangerous methods simply because the individual really didn't have a clear understanding of profitability and financial management. After all, these aren't natural skills that we are born with—they are learned. So if you too have been operating dangerously with your business earnings, it's okay. I'm not going to judge you or shame you! I didn't start keeping track of my deductions with my business until I was nine months in and a week away from my tax deadline. That was a painful learning experience, and I know I'm not the only one to start out that way. I didn't do it because I was lazy or had no desire to do it—I just wasn't educated about what needed to take place and how to manage it.

Here are some examples of poor ways I've seen people handle gross earnings:

- Reinvesting every single dollar back into the business. While it seems like a wise idea, this is a risky thing to do because your business won't yield any immediate benefit. This can quickly lead to resentment and burnout.
- Covering only cost of goods, maybe taxes too, and then keeping the rest as profit. Usually this is super easy to fall into in the start-up phase, when you aren't quite sure if you even really want to have a business or not. You already have the camera, and you know that you need to pay for the print order, but you'll just figure out taxes come tax time. You're used to getting a tax return, so you assume that you probably won't make enough to have to pay any taxes anyway. This is a risky way to handle business. While a hobbyist can totally manage this approach,

IGNORANCE IS NOT BLISS(FUL BUSINESS PRACTICE)

Everything in business is a learning experience, and you aren't at fault for not knowing everything right away. It's easy to change and fix, not the end of the world. You'll learn! But it is still your responsibility to seek out the questions you should be asking and then find someone to teach you how to implement the answers. If you chose to ignore what you need to be doing, then you will see repercussions in your business later because of your disregard for the essentials. Those things will always come back to haunt you whether you believe in them or not.

it's the worst possible way to handle a professional business. Bookkeeping will be a complete nightmare for auditing (should that unluckiness ever befall you), and you will never have any clue if you are making unwise or poor decisions based on number results.

- Landing somewhere in the middle of these two extremes, which is also extreme itself. You know you need to be paying yourself, paying quarterly taxes, bookkeeping, paying back start-up investment, and making money for growth. You *know* these things, but you are caught in a trap where you can't move forward. There's extreme spinning in place. We're creatives—generally speaking, we're not into the numbers—so we avoid this part like the plague. Also, most people in the start-up phase don't realize what their business will demand of them financially to sustain itself and grow. The creative brain loves to think that everything will work itself out; we're optimistic and sometimes, truth be told, not really grounded in reality.

Sorry to be the one to tell you this, folks, but business is where you have to start using the left side of your brain. Just as a left-brained person can exercise the right brain to bring in more creativity—which is generally more appealing—the right-brained person can exercise the left brain and bring on more logic, reason, and strategy. These will never be your dominant skills, but you can employ them if you practice them enough.

The gross-earning calculator

Now that you know what *not* to do, here's what you *should* do: the gross-earning calculator. This tool will give you a clearer picture of what your business will require for you to earn the income you need.

note Please don't send this chart to a business analyst for mathematical accuracy. It's just a rough profit-and-loss tool that can guide you to do things such as redistribute costs to other areas.

This is not an exact science, and it's far from perfect because there are many, many variables. This is just a simple, commonsense budget to see where the money allocations should balance out. After all, 100 percent of your gross income is going to go *some*where—and you need to know where it's going because you are not going to be getting 100 percent to go prop shopping with. I have seen way too many photographers do this when they are starting up: deposit a client's check in the bank and then spend the whole thing on groceries. When times are tough, sure, I get the temptation, but that thinking is going to kill your business. You will pay for it eventually.

Open the gross-earning calculator on your computer, and let's go through this step by step.

When you open the calculator, you'll see two budget plans:

- A healthy budget (**Figure 1.3**), which is the one that you will want if you are on a fast-track plan for your business
- A start-up budget (**Figure 1.4**), which is for you if your business is on a slower track for growth

Seeing as the healthy budget is more focused on growth and sustainability, ideally I want to see you aim for that one, but I included both so you can see how the numbers differ.

Income

First things first: inflow. In cell A2 of the calculator, enter how much you want to earn in personal income. If you followed the steps in "Assessing your work time," you should have this number ready to go (**Figure 1.5**).

I'm going to walk you through this right now to help you figure out exactly how much you want to be earning this next year. Then you can input that number, which influences the next number, which influences the next number...and all the numbers for each category in the gross-earning calculator will be carried forward in the rest of the steps. If you're not clear on this number and need to do some number crunching in your personal finances to see how much you really need to be making, please do so.

note Using the gross-earning calculator is an important step because all the worksheets throughout the book rely on the numbers that are going to be calculated based on your desired income. It'll be easy to tweak as we go, so if you are unsure now, pick a number that you feel is probably closest to what you know it needs to be.

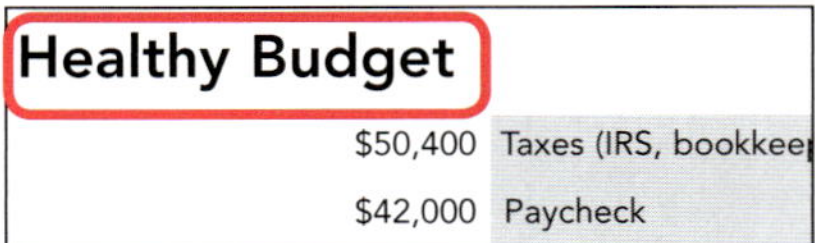

Figure 1.3 A closer look at the gross-earning calculator: a healthy budget

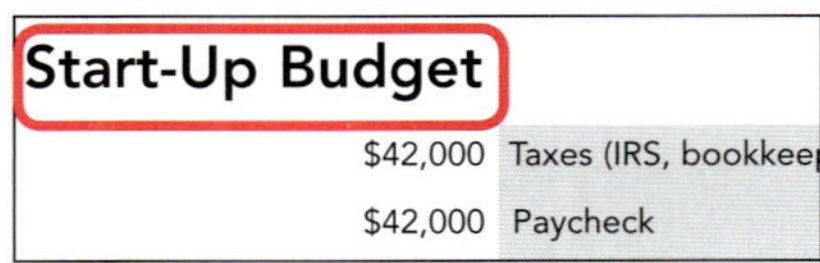

Figure 1.4 A closer look at the gross-earning calculator: a start-up budget

$42,000 Fill in desired personal income goal	How much do you want to earn in personal income?

Figure 1.5 A closer look at the gross-earning calculator: income

Taxes

The first number that you are going to see is the taxes. Why 30 percent, you may ask? We know that taxes are going to be there, and we know that they can be as high as 30 percent. So, it's a safe estimate that will not leave you short come tax time (**Figure 1.6**).

These numbers aren't intended to replace working with a tax professional about how much you should be setting aside. But right now, I just want to give you a no-fail number that you can always calculate into your pricing that will cover your taxes 100 percent of the time. You might even get lucky and have excess, which you can enjoy like a bonus instead of having to deal with panic of not being wisely being prepared for taxes! This is how

ESTIMATED TAXES VS. ACTUAL TAXES

Why estimate that we pay 30 percent of our income in taxes rather than figuring out a more accurate percentage? Because it's really, really hard to factor taxes into your pricing. No business does. It's actually down right impossible unless you consistently sold the exact same number of products every year for the exact same price and had the exact same deductions in your business so you could consistently come up with the exact same percentage. It's just not going to happen. So if you're trying to factor taxes into your pricing, just stop. It's impossible because your numbers will be wrong.

I'm sure I'll get pushback from someone on this topic. I've paid 30 percent before, and it was painful because I was setting aside only 15 percent. So, here's my logic.

Suppose you had previous years where you had barely any profit and you were paying in 15 percent. Then the next year you had explosive profits and still were setting aside only 15 percent. You would be in a lot of pain come tax-filing time when you find out that you are in a higher tax bracket because of that new profit margin.

Here's the scenario in numbers: One year you made $10,000. Fifteen percent of $10,000 is $1500. You set that aside. The next year you made $150,000 and again set aside 15 percent, which is $22,500 (still a painful amount of money to be handing over). But because you earned more and entered a higher tax bracket, you find out that you actually owe 25 percent of $150,000, which is $37,500. That's a difference of $15,000, an excruciating amount to have to come up with at tax time. Total, you're paying $36,000 more in taxes than the previous year!

The year I made this mistake I had to get a loan from the IRS. That's a scary place to be: You have to make large monthly payments, and if you default on a payment, you're in bigger trouble than just defaulting to the bank, which will repossess your house or car. The drama (and debt) can increase thanks to massive penalty fees, increased interest on penalties, forfeiture of tax refunds, seizure of Social Security, a federal tax lien placed on your home, a severely impacted credit report, property seized, forced declaration of bankruptcy, jail time—and having the IRS breathing down your neck for as long as ten years.

large companies handle factoring taxes into products and services, so I think we should follow suit. It works! It's better to have too much set aside than not enough.

Paycheck

The cell right after taxes shows you your paycheck, which is the total you punched in. Yes, more than likely you will make less than the IRS collects in taxes. I encourage you to look at what you're paying to the IRS with gratitude. If you're paying money to the IRS, that means you are in affluence. It's a gift to be able to earn your own livelihood (**Figure 1.7**).

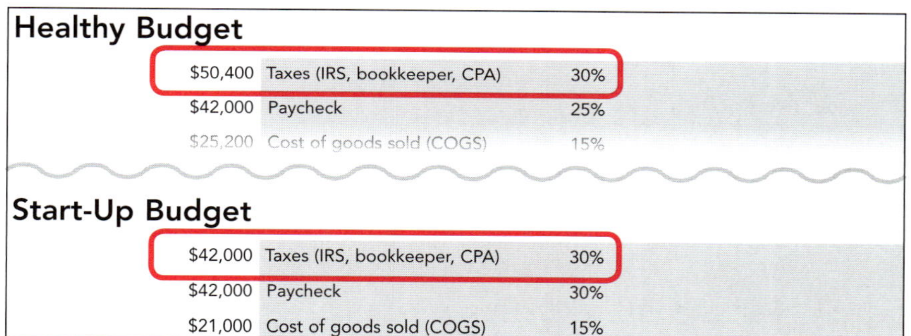

Healthy Budget

$50,400	Taxes (IRS, bookkeeper, CPA)	30%
$42,000	Paycheck	25%
$25,200	Cost of goods sold (COGS)	15%

Start-Up Budget

$42,000	Taxes (IRS, bookkeeper, CPA)	30%
$42,000	Paycheck	30%
$21,000	Cost of goods sold (COGS)	15%

Figure 1.6 A closer look at the gross-earning calculator: taxes

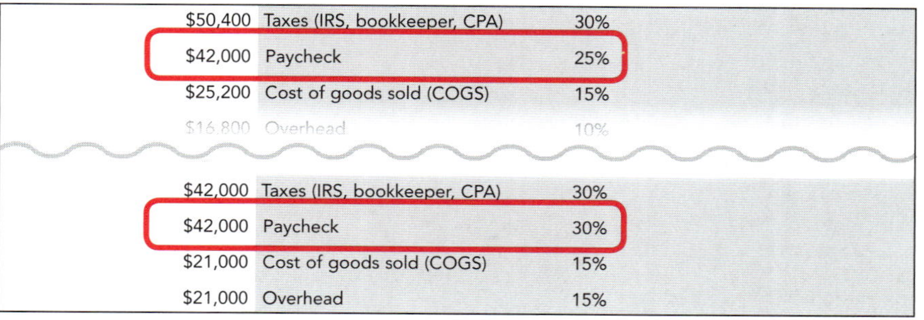

$50,400	Taxes (IRS, bookkeeper, CPA)	30%
$42,000	Paycheck	25%
$25,200	Cost of goods sold (COGS)	15%
$16,800	Overhead	10%

$42,000	Taxes (IRS, bookkeeper, CPA)	30%
$42,000	Paycheck	30%
$21,000	Cost of goods sold (COGS)	15%
$21,000	Overhead	15%

Figure 1.7 A closer look at the gross-earning calculator: income

Cost of goods

The next cell is cost of goods. A big problem area with a lot of photographers is that their cost of goods is so high that there is no margin for profitability (**Figure 1.8**).

There are two ways you can handle this:

- Increase the price for your products and services
- Reduce the cost of goods

We'll talk more about this in Chapter 3 when we build the product catalog. But briefly, the cost of goods is the total breakdown of one-time expenses required to create a product. This includes packaging, printing, and so on. You will always be able to total up what it costs to produce an item when you know the cost of goods.

Overhead

Overhead includes the items that get used several times over—such as cameras, memory cards, Photoshop, regular outsourced editing, and so on—to produce an item (**Figure 1.9**).

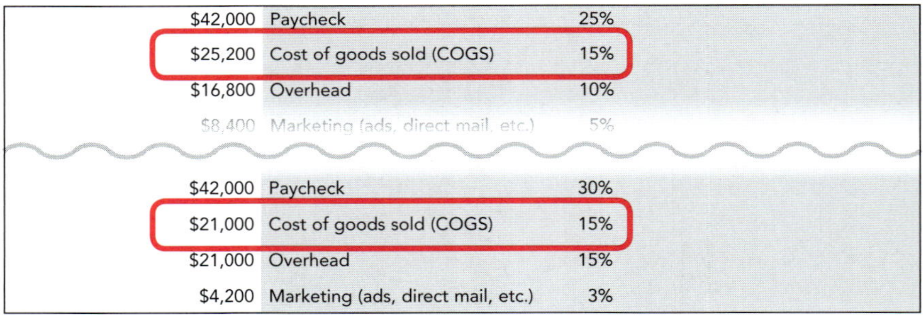

Figure 1.8 A closer look at the gross-earning calculator: cost of goods

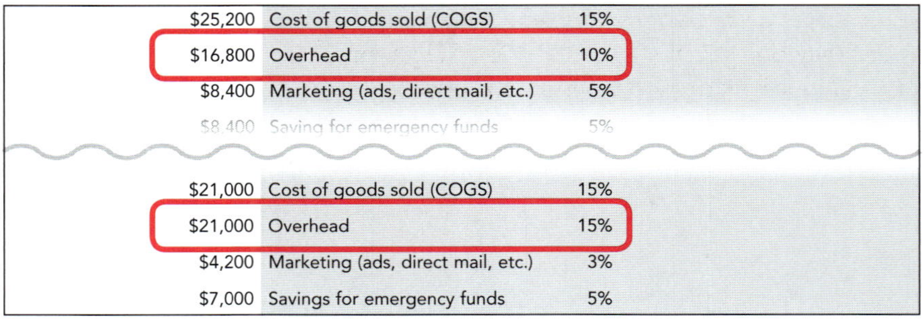

$42,000	Paycheck	25%
$25,200	Cost of goods sold (COGS)	15%
$16,800	Overhead	10%
$8,400	Marketing (ads, direct mail, etc.)	5%

$42,000	Paycheck	30%
$21,000	Cost of goods sold (COGS)	15%
$21,000	Overhead	15%
$4,200	Marketing (ads, direct mail, etc.)	3%

Figure 1.9 A closer look at the gross-earning calculator: overhead

$25,200	Cost of goods sold (COGS)	15%
$16,800	Overhead	10%
$8,400	Marketing (ads, direct mail, etc.)	5%
$8,400	Saving for emergency funds	5%

$21,000	Cost of goods sold (COGS)	15%
$21,000	Overhead	15%
$4,200	Marketing (ads, direct mail, etc.)	3%
$7,000	Savings for emergency funds	5%

This is one area that can be a bit gray. Well, it's completely black and white when your business is self-sufficient but quite hazy when you rely on personal finances to fund your business. All your operating expenses are considered overhead. If you are using personal items for business purposes, you can pay yourself back for those things and claim them as business deductions. But you need to work closely with a CPA on this one to make sure you are handling those things correctly.

tip I always recommend keeping business and personal finances separate. Doing so keeps your business finances much easier to manage.

One important thing I will point out for you with this overhead: If you are making $100,000 gross and your overhead expenses are $10,000 a year, you are going to be on a strict budget with what you are investing in your gadgets and gizmos collection. Having a budget guideline for overhead will help keep you in check so that when you start getting distracted by shiny things—such as actions, props, backdrops, and so on—you will know what your business budget can and can't afford.

And a word of caution: Be aware of all the things you use in your business. A lot of people have said to me "I have really low overhead," and they didn't even realize how much they were using—or were going to be needing—that they didn't factor in.

For example, your computer—even if the family uses it—is overhead. If it dies, your business will need it replaced urgently. That would be a business emergency expense, which counts as overhead because computers need to be replaced regularly, emergency or not. They don't have a very long life.

It's the same for your camera and lenses, which are no longer personal; they are overhead. If they break or die and need to be replaced, that's a business expense to replace, and it's now overhead. So is business insurance, gas for your car driving to sessions, printer ink and paper, your website, and so on. If it's necessary to the function of your business, there's a good chance it's overhead.

It's best to consider these types of items as part of your overhead so that if you need to be saving up for a replacement or upgrade, it is in your budget. That way, not every important replacement has to be taken from your emergency budget. It's a matter of shifting from emergency thinking to preparation thinking and seeing your business tools as overhead.

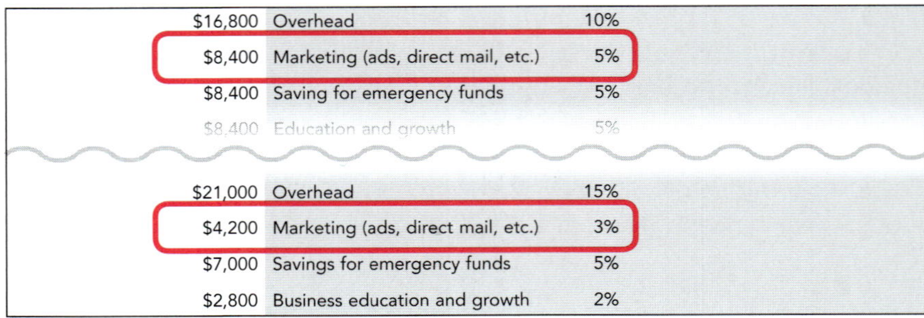

$16,800	Overhead	10%
$8,400	Marketing (ads, direct mail, etc.)	5%
$8,400	Saving for emergency funds	5%
$8,400	Education and growth	5%
$21,000	Overhead	15%
$4,200	Marketing (ads, direct mail, etc.)	3%
$7,000	Savings for emergency funds	5%
$2,800	Business education and growth	2%

Figure 1.10 A closer look at the gross-earning calculator: marketing

Marketing

Marketing (**Figure 1.10**) is not considered overhead. It should be in its own separate category for two reasons:

- It's not completely necessary to the function of your business. You can operate without it, and it's not an urgent need to provide service to your client.
- You should have this budgeted so it's sure to be set aside for its specific purpose. Otherwise, you may be tempted to scrimp on this expense and, as a result, not have it when you need it.

Also, setting aside marketing as a budgeted item makes it easier to track what gets you the most bang for your buck. If you are consistently investing the same amount of money into marketing your business, you will be able to make wiser choices when you see that paying for Facebook ads gives you more return on your investment than Google ads. Or you can see whether you really can afford that ad in the local magazine. Having a specific amount allocated for marketing will help ensure that you are always intentionally focused on growth—even if overhead expenses fluctuate for the month, your focus on growth will always be consistent.

Emergency funds

Emergency funds (**Figure 1.11**) cover anything, such as the following:

- Holiday-season craziness, when you take on more clients than you thought you could handle and now need someone to help you package and deliver an order
- Broken equipment

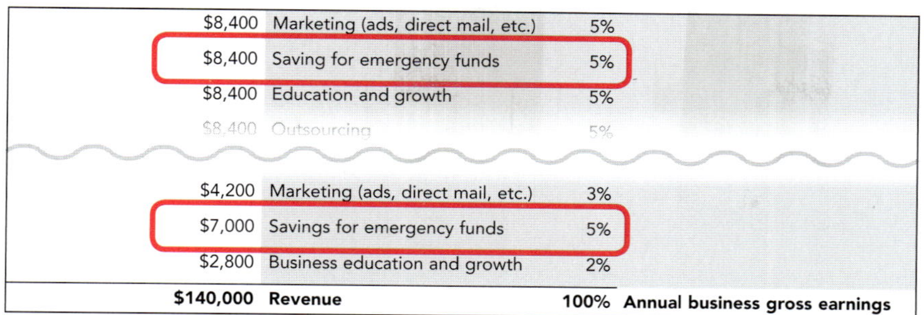

$8,400	Marketing (ads, direct mail, etc.)	5%	
$8,400	Saving for emergency funds	5%	
$8,400	Education and growth	5%	
$8,400	Outsourcing	5%	

$4,200	Marketing (ads, direct mail, etc.)	3%	
$7,000	Savings for emergency funds	5%	
$2,800	Business education and growth	2%	
$140,000	**Revenue**	**100%**	**Annual business gross earnings**

Figure 1.11 A closer look at the gross-earning calculator: emergency funds

- Hiring a tech person after your website crashes
- Having to refund an upset client who is disappointed in their order and the only way to satisfy them is giving their money back

Crazy stuff happens. You should always be focused on setting aside some cash so when you are up to your eyeballs in editing, your kids are all home sick with the flu, and your inbox is overflowing, you have the money to pay for help.

Don't forget: You take out; you put back in. If you dip into your emergency stash, pay yourself back as quickly as you can. Also, wise financial planning includes having three to six months of operating expenses at all times. So if you have quite a bit of savings adding up, don't cut back—one day, that chunk will come in handy, and you'll be thankful you had it set aside.

note Most people are resistant to saving, but you must save emergency funds. I don't need to beat you over the head about why this is important. You know it's important. Now it's now just a matter of treating it like it is. IMPORTANT.

Education and growth

This is a category that I would never, ever skimp on. For some, it seems like a high percentage of earnings to go toward education. But I will tell you straight: Education is just as important, if not more so, than marketing (**Figure 1.12**).

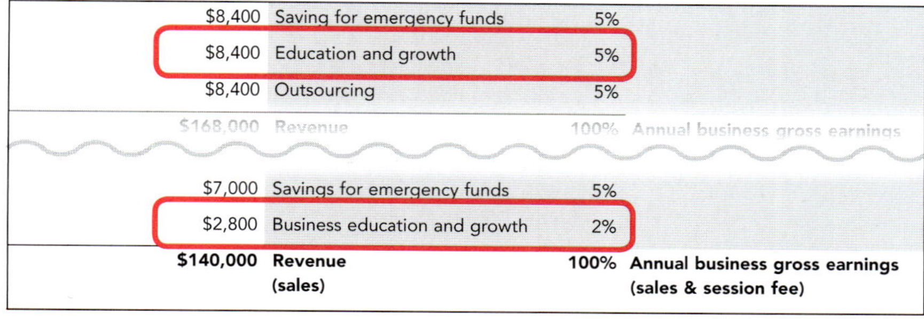

$8,400	Saving for emergency funds	5%	
$8,400	Education and growth	5%	
$8,400	Outsourcing	5%	
$168,000	Revenue	100%	Annual business gross earnings

$7,000	Savings for emergency funds	5%	
$2,800	Business education and growth	2%	
$140,000	**Revenue (sales)**	**100%**	**Annual business gross earnings (sales & session fee)**

Figure 1.12 A closer look at the gross-earning calculator: education and growth

Tip My rule of thumb: If you need money, learn business. If you don't need money, have fun growing your art. Rarely will your clients see quality improvements in your work, even if you do feel so much better about what you are producing, so improving your work will rarely yield more money.

I'm going to be prejudice and say that I believe business education is all you need...but some people do need some additional photography education. Just make sure that you keep your balance and always favor the business side when you are needing financial growth.

Outsourcing

This is one area a start-up business can't always afford to include, and sometimes you have to hustle working more hours than you will get a return on. But being able to outsource some work should always be your goal (**Figure 1.13**).

As I mentioned earlier in the chapter, outsourcing can range from housekeeping to editing to virtual assistant to second shooter...you name it. You can spin your wheels and give up sleep trying to do everything on your own, or you can circulate the money so that you can free up time to do what you do best—or just catch up on sleep.

A healthy business builds a support system to maintain itself and to keep the flow growing and thriving. You'll never master all areas of creation, management, and administration. You will need to bring in others to assist you for you to continue to grow in your zone of genius.

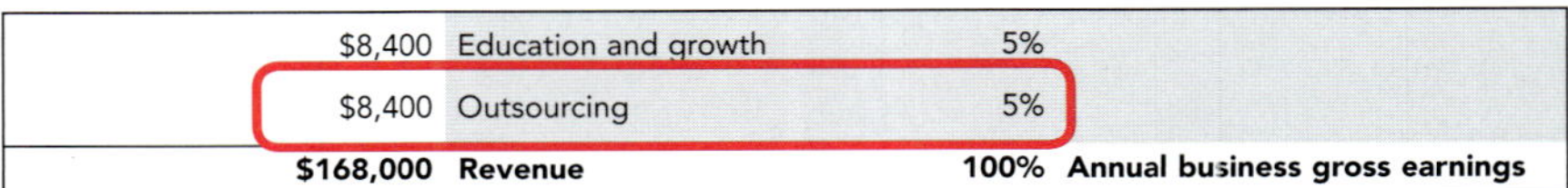

$8,400	Education and growth	5%	
$8,400	Outsourcing	5%	
$168,000	**Revenue**	**100%**	**Annual business gross earnings**

Figure 1.13 A closer look at the gross-earning calculator: outsourcing

Doing the math

This is when I really want you to keep an open mind. Don't overthink. Just go with your first instincts. More than likely you're going to let fear talk you out of taking the necessary steps (namely, going through the worksheets in this chapter step by step). But just right now, go through the process and look at it with hopeful expectation, positive thinking, and optimism. You may or may not be ready mentally and emotionally to take the needed leap. That's okay. But don't immediately shoot down what you know needs to happen or you will get discouraged.

With that said, let's walk through filling in Your Numbers Bible, one line at a time.

tip Get these business days and hours established on your email autoresponder, on your website, and in your calendar. It will feel so good to have your whole year planned ahead! That way you can always make sure you have dedicated time for your business without overscheduling, overcommitting, and trying to squeeze in business time. Remember, business comes first, and then you can play with the rest of the time as it comes.

Your hourly value

1. Earlier in this chapter you looked at your calendar and determined how many weeks per year you had available for work. That is going to go on line A of Your Numbers Bible worksheet.
2. Go down to the math equation under line C and, where it says "A," enter the number you have in line A.
3. In line B, enter how many days per week you are dedicating to your business and then add that number in the math equation where it says "B."
4. In line C, enter how many hours per day you'll work and then add that to the math equation where it says "C."
5. Now multiply your weeks (A) times your days (B) times your hours (C). Your total is your annual business hours you are available, line D.

   Bear in mind that this is an estimate—you may work more, you may work less. You don't have to commit to these numbers right here and now; they are merely guidelines to keep you realistic about what's a reasonable workload and what would be insanity to attempt.
6. For line F, divide your annual gross income (which you got from your annual gross-earnings calculator) (on line E) by your total annual business hours available (line D).

   The result: your hourly value, or what your time is worth for you to be able to achieve your sales goals.
7. For the next two lines, halve your business hours (line D) and dedicate them to your clients in line G and your business in line H.

note You may need to go back over this to refine the numbers, but I want to go through the whole process now, even if you are just initially guessing on some of the numbers. Let's continue.

YOUR NUMBERS BIBLE

Your hourly value

A. **20____ (year) weeks available:**

____

B. **Business days per week:**

____

C. **Business hours per day:**

____

D. **A ______ × B ______ × C ______ =**
Annual business hours available

____

E. **Annual gross income:**

____

F. **E ______ ÷ D ______ =**
Hourly value:

____

G. **Client hours 50%:**

____

H. **Business hours 50%:**

____

Clients per year

Estimated hours per client:

- Customer service & communication:

  ____
- Shooting: ______________________________
- Editing: ______________________________
- Sales: ______________________________
- Packaging: ______________________________
- Delivering: ______________________________

I. **Total hours per client:**

____

J. **G (available client hours) ______ ÷**
I (hours per client)______ =
Clients per year: ________________

K. **E (annual gross income) ______ ÷**
J (clients per year) ______ =
____________ (gross income per client)

L. **Session fee (see Table 1.1):**

____

M. **K (gross per client)______ –**
L (session fee) ______ =
MOR: ________________________

Worksheet summary

A. 20____ weeks available:

____

B. Business days per week:

____

C. Hours per day:

____

D. Annual business hours available:

____

E. Annual gross income:

____

F. Hourly value:

____

G. Available client hours:

____

H. Available business hours:

____

I. Total hours per client:

____

J. Maximum clients per year:

____

K. Minimum client earning:

____

L. Session fee:

____

M. Minimum order requirement:

____

MAKE EVERY HOUR COUNT

When I figured out my hourly value, I was shocked by what my time was worth—or what I needed to earn hourly to be profitable. I put that number on a sticky note on my laptop for a while so that every time I was distracted by Facebook or some other online rabbit hole, I would reprimand myself: "Alicia, that hour just cost you $300. Was it worth it to you? And where are you going to make that up?"

Good mental reminders, even if they're just sticky notes, help to keep you in check when you are wanting to wander. Instead, you need to be focused, dedicated to the hours you are giving to your business and making sure that you are spending those hours doing valuable things.

There always needs to be balance in your business. You may not always be spending exactly 50 percent of the time with your clients and 50 percent on management and administration, but it's a pretty good balance to strive for. I even recommend scheduling specific hours for clients and specific hours for marketing and education. Doing so helps maintain that balance so you never have the excuse that you don't have time to grow. Everything is on your plate because you said yes to it. So start saying yes to your business.

Maximum client capacity

Now let's figure out how many clients you can handle.

1. Write down how many hours you spend with your client, broken down by customer service and communications, shooting, editing, and so on.
2. Add these up, and you have your total hours per client in line I.
3. In line J, enter your client hours (from line G) and divide that number by your average client hours (line I).

   The result is exactly how many clients you should estimate to bring into your business for the year.
4. In line K, enter your annual gross income (from line E) and divide it by your maximum number of clients per year (line J).

   The result is the minimum that you need to bring in, in gross sales, per client. This will include your session fee and sales goal.

note This is reverse engineering, folks. We aren't trying to cram as many clients as possible into our life. We are creating a healthy and manageable business and then determining the pricing that it requires to achieve that.

Session fee

Now, to determine your session fee, use the handy-dandy Session Fee Cheat Sheet (**Table 1.1**) to see what session fee best fits the sales goal you are looking to meet. On line L, enter the session fee that meets your sales goal.

Table 1.1 Session Fee Cheat Sheet

SESSION FEE	SALES GOAL
$100	Less than $300 total
$150	$300–$1500
$151–$250	$1000–$1500
$251–$350	$1500–$3000
$350–$450	$3000–$9000

Minimum order requirement

One of the best business decisions I ever made was putting in a minimum order requirement (MOR). Setting a minimum fee per order builds security and profitability into your rates.

Another purpose of the MOR is that it simply becomes a deterrent for someone who doesn't have the budget to spend. When your MOR is listed on your website, you eliminate tire-kickers wanting to know what your prices are when they're probably not really committed to hiring you anyway.

Now that you understand the concept of an MOR, back to the worksheet! To determine your MOR (line M), simply subtract your session fee (L) from your gross income per client (line K). *Voila*!

Whew, you did it! I know how hard number crunching is, and you did great! Remember that these numbers are not set in stone, so don't feel like you need to make sure that they are perfect before moving forward. They may need to change as you reevaluate the direction you are heading in, which we will be covering more as we talk about your ideal client and whether these numbers will work for that person.

MY MOR

Early in my business I was averaging $125 per session, and my largest order was for $250. I was exhausted, overworked, and underpaid. I had to take charge or else I would lose both my business and my sanity.

So, I sat down and started crunching numbers. I reverse engineered my pricing based on the factors of how much money I needed for personal income and how much that would require my business to produce and divided that by how many sessions I was physically capable of taking on.

At the time, my calculations told me that I had to talk away with at least $400 to meet that minimum earning. So, $400 became my MOR, and after that time, I didn't have a single session not provide the money that I needed in order to profit. With each client, I was bringing in $550 between the session fee and sale.

But the problem that I began to encounter was that I needed more to cover more than just taxes, cost of goods, and personal income. I needed to have money for marketing, education, savings, and overhead.

As my needs increased, I had to bump up my minimum order requirement to $500 per client and increase my session fee from $125 to $250. Then, I was bringing in a minimum of $750 with every client. And the fascinating thing was I wasn't even having clients spend the minimum anymore because I built my collections to start at $900, and the majority of my clients were going for the lowest or middle package and sometimes even the highest.

So, having a MOR built sustainability to my business and maximized the profit in my collections. The strategy worked like a charm—I was meeting our financial needs as well as my business needs.

2

THE IDEAL CLIENT AND YOUR MARKETPLACE

The ideal client. Probably one of the biggest frustrations that I encounter working with photographers is trying to figure out who the heck this person is.

This is generally a marketing topic, but I think it really needs to be a pricing topic first because it helps you understand what your clients are willing to spend, and their wants and needs, before you try to sell them what you *think* they want or need. Let's skip the assumptions and go searching for the facts!

In this chapter, we'll focus on identifying your ideal client, as well as how to get into his or her head. Doing so will help you begin to better understand who your ideal client is and to shape your pricing and products to best serve this person—all while making sure that your business is achieving profitability and sustainability.

Designing your ideal-client avatar

note If you aren't familiar with the term *avatar*, it's an icon or figure representing a particular person—not an air-bender or really tall blue person.

Marketing courses often recommend that you design your ideal-client avatar, specifying the person's name, age, religion, income, lifestyle, and so on. All of this is important information to know so that you can visualize and humanize the person you are trying to reach. If you just try to market to someone who "values your art and wants to pay you," it's really hard to know where to go find that person, how to talk to him or her, what he or she values, what he or she already spent money on, and more. So for you to have an idea where to focus your marketing energy, you need to get in the head of your ideal client by designing a hypothetical lifestyle for him or her. (Doing so will also help you avoid the pronoun gymnastics seen here. For simplicity moving forward, I'll alternate between referring to our unknown ideal as "him" or "her" by section.)

The price point of affordability

tip I always find that when you put yourself in a client's shoes, you better understand his thinking. So to do this, you have to have a relatable struggle or situation—even if it's not exactly the same, it'll help you gain perspective.

In creating the ideal-client avatar, the element that is always missing is the answer to this all-important question: "Can he afford you?" Note that this is not the same as his income level. Some of my lowest-paying clients were millionaires, and some of my highest-paying ones couldn't even be considered middle class. Although someone's income level does play a role, it's still not a determining factor in whether that person can afford you. Look beyond elements like household income; focus more on the *price point of affordability*—how much is the client willing to spend to get what he wants?

Have you ever looked at something that you couldn't afford at the time but logged it into your memory bank with a plan to buy it as soon as you had the funds? That was something that fit into your price point of affordability.

If someone was trying to sell that product and looked at you only if you currently had the finances, then technically you wouldn't be an ideal client, right? But, if someone looked at you as a potential client because you had that price point of affordability in your mind—that willingness to spend the money if you had it—you would be an ideal client. It would be worthwhile to continue marketing energy toward you so that you could continually be reminded of how much you want that thing and could make it a priority to either save for it or jump on the opportunity as soon as you had the finances.

When reaching out to your ideal client, marketing efforts aren't always going to yield instant results. The ideal client has long-term value. I've purchased several things in my lifetime that I first purchased mentally, letting them simmer in my mind for a few years before I actually invested the money and owned the things. If you have an Amazon wish list, you know what I'm talking about.

That is what marketing to an ideal client looks like: The person may not be the right fit right now, but he would like to be someday. What someone is willing to pay you may be completely different than what someone can currently afford.

Market to clients, not budgets

When you market to your ideal clients, they can instantly see the value of paying you $1500. These are the type of people who swoon over your work and generally say "I wish I could afford you" in a way that doesn't come across as "You're too expensive."

Unfortunately, these people are not in the financial place to be able to pay you right now. But their price points of affordability are still ideal because they see the value in you. They are comfortable with that number, and they will log you into their memory banks as being a "someday I hope I can have that." Even though right now they can't pay you, it does not mean that you have lost them as clients. You can still market to them, as they are still a match for the price point of affordability. Don't completely rule them out.

To understand why, consider a handbag analogy. Almost every woman owns a handbag, but what the purchaser is willing to pay can vary hugely from one woman to the next. Let's say someone predetermines that she would never, ever spend $5000 on a Louis Vuitton bag because she feels that's a ridiculous price to pay for a handbag. Even if her income increased dramatically, she has already determined that she cannot afford that bag because she doesn't see the value—she has a lower price point of affordability. When her income increases, she isn't going to go Louis Vuitton shopping because *her ability to pay for the bag doesn't change her value of it*. It doesn't change her price point of affordability.

Now consider someone who is struggling financially and swoons over the idea of toting that logo around someday. Even if she can't afford it currently, the bag is still within her price point of affordability. As soon as her financial situation changes and she can pay the asking price, she is going to see the handbag as affordable—and she's going to buy it.

note The price point of affordability is going to look different for different photographers, because each of you is going to have different income goals, hourly availability, client capacities, and so on. You all have unique situations that you'll factor into the specific business model you are creating.

The point is that you still want to attract people who may not be able to pay you right now. If you continue to market to them and foster a relationship with them over the years, as soon as they do have the finances, they will hire you—and your marketing efforts will pay off. The income situation for most people generally shifts and changes, and rarely does anyone stay in one place. That's why you want to market to the price point of affordability, not the income level.

Prequalifying clients: can they afford you?

When you ask whether a potential client can afford you, the answer is not a simple yes or no. When you are creating your ideal-client avatar, of course he can afford you—you're designing him to afford you! Obviously.

But what is his price point of affordability? That's what you need to understand and establish before you can flesh out your ideal client. It should always be step 1 in designing your ideal-client avatar. You need ways to prequalify your clients—that is, to see whether they fit within *your* price point of affordability.

In Chapter 1, "Getting Started," you determined that number. First, you calculated your minimum order requirement (MOR), the amount you needed to make per client to be profitable and sustainable (refer to line M in the "Your Numbers Bible" worksheet). Using Table 1.1, you then determined the best session fee for you based on an industry standard of what clients spend on average based on the type of session they purchase. These session fee price points and the sales that they average have been pretty darn consistent in all of the people with whom I have worked and interviewed over the last eight years, as well as what I experienced in my own business.

When clients first encounter your business, they aren't thinking of all that they are going to get for the money, for example, how many 8x10s and digital files they are going to get. All they really want to know immediately is how much money it is going to cost to work with you. Be up front with your session fee and MOR to prequalify clients and avoid negative feelings later.

Some clients will move forward and hire you without this specific information, but you can guarantee that it's still a question in their minds when they come in contact with you. And these people, who hire you without

HONESTY = TRUST = REPEAT CUSTOMERS

When you are up front and honest with your clients, you build trust. Trusting clients are the ones who know how much they are going to spend—and if the experience was amazing for them from start to finish, they will definitely be coming back and telling their friends about you because you met or exceeded their expectations. They may not know up front exactly what they are going to get for the money, but they are willing to spend it because they trust you—and then you have the opportunity to meet or exceed what they consider valuable.

When clients first encounter you, they aren't going to be emotionally attached to your products. You are selling them an idea, and that idea needs to be something they are comfortable with. If they don't know exactly what to expect, they will establish their own expectations, which leads to dissatisfaction because you won't be on the same page.

fully knowing what they are getting, are going to be the clients who either wheel and deal as they go along—asking for discounts, humphing at the prices, being demanding for requests because they want to make sure they get substantial bang for their buck, and so on—or they are going to walk away feeling yucky because they spent more than they imagined they would. When you push your clients to a place of discomfort, you end up dealing with a ton of negative emotions. For instance, clients may feel scared of making the wrong decision and wasting money, guilty for spending more than they expected, ashamed that they weren't aware of what everything was going to cost, and embarrassed to look cheap. Even if they love their images, they won't be coming back. The overall walk-away emotion is what determines how they feel about returning.

If you present a potential client with only a session fee, without mentally selling him the minimum order requirement, you are being elusive. Furthermore, selling just a session isn't really that valuable. As a photographer *you* think it's valuable, because you know all of the work that goes into it. But to the client, if all he did was hire you for the session, it's not that valuable to him at all. He gets nothing in return for the money because simply giving him your time gives him no tangible benefit. Clients aren't going to thank you for pointing a camera at them, hand you money, and be satisfied. It's like paying for a show that they don't get to see.

The problem that you will encounter when you sell just the session fee first and then focus on presenting image prices later is having to work twice as hard to convince clients to buy. Once you've convinced them to give you money for the session, then having to convince them to give you *more*

> ### WAIT TO DISPLAY YOUR WARES
>
> You might be thinking, but shouldn't I first show them all the things they can buy?
>
> Yes, you will need to do this eventually. But it doesn't factor into your clients determining whether you are within their price points of affordability. Let me explain.
>
> If you know that you are comfortable with spending only $200 on a handbag, the features and benefits of owning a $5000 handbag don't matter—you just know the bag is not for you. You know the price point and that it's more than you are willing to spend, whether you have the cash for it or not. You set your own mental price point of affordability, which has nothing to do with what you get for the money.
>
> Your clients are the same way. They're not going to be mentally calculating all the things they can get from you. Although you may encounter some people who want to crunch every number for exactly everything that they can possibly get, most aren't obsessed immediately about how many 8x10s they will receive for your price. They predetermined a budget in their heads before they even considered approaching you. They don't need to know all the features and benefits to see whether you're within their price points of affordability.

money in the sale of products is very tough. From a marketing and sales perspective, selling images separate from a session is super hard because, in essence, you are selling two products or services—and separate products are expected to have separate results, correct?

So by stating your session fee and MOR up front, you are able to get your clients to mentally lump together these two things, and they can determine whether you fit their price points of affordability. The session fee, then, is just looked at as a deposit and not as a separate experience. Right away clients can determine "Am I cool with this?" and see immediate value or "Do I feel uncomfortable and I don't think I could get anything that would be worth that price no matter how amazing the experience is?" By presenting the session fee and minimum order requirement together, you then are attracting ideal clients who are looking with their price points of affordability. When they hire you with the awareness of what they need to spend ahead of time, they will be far more relaxed and excited about the process because they aren't having to deal with money shockers. Get that out of the way immediately and then can focus on providing them value.

Pricing on your website attracts ideal clients

Establishing your price point with your session fee and minimum order requirement is the place to start. The next step is to be transparent about your pricing by providing it on your website. By clearly stating this information, your website copy can help you prequalify clients—attracting your ideal kind and deterring the wrong kind. Build into your copy all your features and benefits so that clients understand exactly all that they will be getting from start to finish working with you.

I go to websites all the time that do not include pricing. Perhaps the owner doesn't want other photographers stealing the pricing, or maybe the owner frequently changes pricing and doesn't want to update the site constantly. But here's the problem: The lack of pricing prevents serious people from inquiring. No one likes vague—Is the website still in business? Do the prices constantly change? Are the prices too high to list?—so you need to have basic pricing on your website. For clients, seeing the numbers is actually less intimidating than contacting someone with no frame of reference. Realizing too late that you're wasting a photographer's time because she is completely beyond your budget is an unpleasant feeling all around. Not wanting to be "that guy," clients who may fit your price points will hesitate to reach out to you. It's the fear that stops them.

Stop that fear by including a separate business page on your website that explains a session in detail, as well as your session fee and MOR. Yes, it is possible that someone could steal your website copy and your idea, but you legally can protect yourself by having a lawyer send out a cease-and-desist order if you encounter copyright infringement. The money you'll bring in thanks to the trust factor you'll establish with clients should cover your cost easily.

note For more information on polishing your website copy to increase your chances of connecting with your ideal client, check out Chapter 4, "The Grand Reveal," as well as my eBook Website Copy Workshop (www.profitfirstphotography.com/website-copy-workshop/).

The courage to turn away

It takes a lot of courage getting comfortable with prequalifying your clients this way because you'll get freaked out when you think about all the potential clients you are losing (who actually weren't in the price point of affordability). But you have to go through a process of elimination when you are targeting your ideal client—and that means ridding yourself of the ones who cannot give you a profit or sustain you.

KNOW YOUR PROFITABILITY MODEL

My goal for this book is to give you a better understanding of all of the elements that work together for profitability and sustainability. As you are beginning to see, there is so much more to it than just presenting a price list and selling prints.

How you price yourself and how you stay consistent with that pricing is your branding. For example, department store photo studios, like JC Penny or Target, offer basic quality at low price points but thrive on high-volume business. Boutique photographers who offer high-quality portraits for higher session fees and MORs rely on a lower volume of sales. The clients of both models have budgets and, more importantly, price points of affordability but have different mentalities and want factors. You need to understand what goes into a client's want factor and then determine whether it's in alignment with what you provide. To understand what I mean, consider two successful jeans companies: Old Navy and 7 For All Mankind.

Strictly a low-sale/high-volume manufacturer, Old Navy keeps its prices for jeans low and relatively constant over the years. The company knows that its ideal client is willing to spend a specific dollar amount and no more for its commodity, in this case jeans. Rather than raise prices, Old Navy might reduce quality, service, or other expenses to maintain its price points and, in turn, its profitability and sustainability. That is how every low-sale/high-volume pricing system works: You cut corners in quality and service to keep the price point what you know your ideal client is willing to spend.

Clients of 7 For All Mankind, a luxury jean company that features high sales and low volume, on the other hand, is willing to spend more to get the features it wants—fabulous fit, quality materials, personal care from salespeople, and the intangible of feeling amazing and confident in the product. An incremental price increase won't alienate these clients because they're shopping more for results than price. Clients of luxury brands and boutiques know that they get what they pay for and are more suspect of deep discounts, which might imply flaws in quality or fit.

You need to evaluate where your business and your clients align on the commodity to luxury spectrum. If you know, for example, that you need to make $2000 per client to make your business sustainable but don't know how that will be possible with what you are currently doing, you need to change one thing or another. You can increase the value of what you are providing and how you serve your client to make that $2000 have greater worth to your client (luxury jeans), or you can lower your prices and you decrease your cost of goods by selling only what fits that price point (commodity jeans).

A lot of people tell me that they would rather have low-paying clients than no paying clients, so when they are hurting for money, they don't turn away clients. I get that, especially when money is tight. But I also know that the rationale behind that is based on fear, not on wise business practice. If you are struggling to bring in clients, working with a low-paying client will take time away from your focusing on marketing, growing your business, and attracting your ideal client. If you focus on just the here and now, you will stay stuck forever because you won't ever have the time or energy to work on attracting the right clients.

It's a vicious cycle and one that you have to break by accepting that you *will* lose people and you *will* have to turn away some. But in so doing, you are

- Readying your business for the clients who are going to pay you what your business needs to be profitable and sustainable
- Preparing for people who are a good fit for your business
- Finding the clients who will come to you repeatedly over the years and tell their friends about you

This bigger-picture thinking doesn't allow fear to immobilize you from taking that next step forward!

Making these business decisions is not changing who you are; you aren't looking down on the person who can't afford you and setting yourself up as a superior. You are simply building a business to serve the people who can afford to pay you for your time and energy and who see the value in what you do. That's just being a wise businessperson.

Please do not allow fear tell you that you are prideful, arrogant, or hurting people's feelings when you make these business decisions. As long as your heart is in the right place, these feelings are just fear telling you that the pain in growth is not worth doing what is necessary.

WHY THEY REALLY HIRE YOU

Don't let your price point freak you out, especially if it's out of your current budget. You will never be your ideal client. That doesn't mean that you can cater only to people who are within or below your current budget. I know that you may struggle with the intimidation factor of working with people who you don't relate to, but don't let fear completely block the reasoning ability in this situation. These people aren't hiring you because of your lifestyle—they are hiring you for the quality of your work and how you serve their emotional and physical needs.

I have to be perfectly honest: Your audience really doesn't care about you. They are hiring you because they care about themselves, and you have something that they want—if not need—to be emotionally satisfied. It has nothing to do with just wanting your art and to support you because you are an amazing human being.

Same goes for my business—people don't hire me because they want to spend time with Alicia, basking in my presence.

I'm hired by photographers who have a need. They care about themselves, and they want the experience and knowledge that I have because it improves their lives. They don't hire me just because they want to support my business and to let me live the life that I want. They really don't care about that part. It's nothing personal—they just want what I have, which can help them with what they are lacking.

If you bought this book, you'll understand that. You trust me, but you don't care what car I drive, what I wear, or where I shop. Those things were not factors at all in determining whether I'd be a good fit for helping you with your business. So please, do not believe that you have to fit a certain lifestyle to be able to market to it!

Four key characteristics of the ideal client

Your ideal client, or as I like to say *your business soulmate*, must embody four key characteristics.

- He meets your needed price points and can bring you profitability.
- He finds your business to be the perfect solution for his problem.
- He is a sustainable client who will keep coming back to you.
- He constantly recommends you to his friends.

Notice the list didn't include anything about an ideal amount the client should spend. Although it's fabulous to set goals for the amount your clients should spend, you don't need to look at your ideal person as the one who buys your biggest package and tons of extra stuff. That's an *amazing* client, but it isn't your ideal client. Your ideal client is the one that reflects 80 percent of your clients, leaving the other 20 percent of your business to bring in amazing clients.

Nor is your ideal customer necessarily the person who just loves, loves, *loves* you. The problem is that no matter how much someone loves you, if she can't pay the rates that your business needs to sustain itself, you have to adjust something. Building a business on clients who can't afford you is going to run you into the ground, and you will find out quickly that you are basically paying to photograph your clients. It may sound obvious, but if there is no profit in your business, you are throwing away your time and money.

How to design your ideal client

To complete the picture beyond the four key characteristics, you can (and should) use the following worksheet to further flesh out these ideal-client qualities. If your business could have only one customer that repeats over and over, pays your full session pricing without discounts, and comes to you with needs that you know you can provide, this is your business soulmate. You'd be happy to do business with this ideal client over and over again because your business could sustain itself on this type of person if every single client who came to you was like your ideal client.

UNDERSTANDING THE CHEAPIE

We've all worked with him and he's not ideal: The Cheapie is the client who expects better treatment than your already awesome service but treats you like he's doing you a favor by paying you $200 for $1000 worth of merchandise. The Cheapie will barter and negotiate to lower your pricing with no regard to you as a business owner. The Cheapie will protest the extra fees that you charge when he demands for rush shipping or retouching 25 pounds away from his waistline with the Liquify tool.

Overflowing with a clear sense of entitlement and an unrealistic sense of what his budget should be able to buy, the Cheapie is deal seeker who lives for the thrill of thrift. Cheapies get a high from what they save, not for what they actually get. Cheapies also show up 20 minutes late to a session because they do not understand the value of someone else's time.

The Cheapie is a far cry from the individual who hires you with a budget of $800 and expects $800 worth of artwork in return. Clients who purchase your minimum order aren't necessarily cheap. The minimum may be all that they could afford, but they'd rather pay your price for fewer quality prints than hire someone else for a lot less money and get a lot more prints that they don't love. These clients know your value and are willing to pay what they can afford.

When you do find a cheapie, do not let that individual devalue your time or fall prey to his multitude of ways of convincing you just how expensive your work happens to be. Don't let them give you business advice. Know that you cannot be profitable if you let the Cheapie alter your business practice. Refuse to wheel and deal. The price is the price.

Recognize that you can't make Cheapies value what you do. You can only show them how you are valuable and let them determine whether that is what they are willing to pay for—or not. It's okay for both of you to not be the perfect fit; you can't be for everyone. It's okay to let some go that aren't an ideal customer. Communicate your value based on what you *know* your clients want and need in their lives.

WHO IS YOUR IDEAL CLIENT?

Male or female? ______________________________

Married or single? ______________________________

Any kids? How many? ______________________________

Any pets? ______________________________

Occupation? ______________________________

Annual income? ______________________________

Any hobbies? ______________________________

____

____

Where does the person live? ______________________________

____

____

What kind of house does the person have? ______________________________

____

____

What kind of car does the person drive? ______________________________

____

____

What does the person do for entertainment? ______________________________

____

____

Where does the person shop? ______________________________

____

____

Where does the person like to eat out? ______________________________

____

____

Where does the person vacation? ______________________________

____

____

____

What kind of websites does the person spend time on? ______________________________

____

____

____

Is the person into social media? Blogs? ______________________________

____

____

____

How is the person's house decorated? ______________________________

____

____

____

What is the person's favorite clothing store? ______________________________

____

____

____

How does the person fill free time? ______________________________

____

____

____

____

____

____

Now, I want you to consider all the information in the "Who Is Your Ideal Client" worksheet and tell me all you know about this person. Describe your ideal in detail so well that you can truly think like and understand this person. This is your business soulmate, and you need to know your soulmate intimately. Remember that your soulmate is *not* you, although you may have similarities or common interests. Give this person a unique name, age, and address.

Along the way, remember that photography is not an essential in life. Unlike breathing or food, it's not a key to survival. That means when clients hire a portrait or wedding photographer, they are doing it based on emotions and not based on survival instincts.

The mom who hires you for her son's senior portraits isn't merely fulfilling an item on the senior-year check list. She's continuing a tradition that's emotionally significant. But what are her emotions? Perhaps she wants to make this final year with her "baby" last or to celebrate the man he's becoming. Maybe she wants to show off to all the other moms to show everyone her crowning achievement: her son.

Likewise, the business man needing headshots needs more than just a quick photo. After all, he could turn his smartphone around and snap a decent picture. He wants to be respected. He wants to convey power and strength. He wants to present himself to the world as a professional. All of these reasons come from the heart.

Tip When filling out the worksheet "A Deeper Dive into Your Ideal Client," use information from the past client surveys discussed in the section "How to survey your ideal client" to deduce the answers instead of assuming them. You will better understand how to answer the worksheet's questions, if you hear feedback from real clients.

Does one of these sound like your ideal client? If not, what does? Use the next worksheet to dive deep into why the client wants to hire you and why that person wants what only you can provide.

Now that you have described your business soulmate, you know why he or she wants to hire you and how you are going to improve that person's life. With this information you can build your business and further tailor your website copy to reach out to that person. You'll be able to speak to your ideal clients through more than just beautiful imagery. You'll be able to market specifically through everything that you do in your business, because every element draws them to you—from design to shooting style, pricing to session descriptions, your blog to the way you present your contact information.

Survey your past and potential clients

If you struggled with the ideal-client worksheets, don't despair. It's often easier to define your business soulmate when you can use information and data that comes from actual clients, instead of just assuming what you *think* your clients want and need. After years of trying to create that perfect person, I decided to reach out to some of my excellent past clients and just ask them for feedback. Suddenly, I didn't have to assume anymore—I got an outline of my ideal client's thoughts directly from them, and it was so much better than anything I could have put together. In the section that follows, you'll find a sample survey that asks for all the information you need to flesh out the previous ideal-client avatar worksheet. Together these tools will help you use the language that your current clients speak to reach out to more clients like them.

If you want to get into their brains and understand how your ideal clients think and what they value, make a regular practice of surveying all your past clients who possess the four key characteristics of an ideal client. The results will help you continually refine your business through an evolving understanding of what your clients really want and how you can better serve them.

COLLECT, THEN MARKET

People tell me all the time how what I teach resonates with them personally—like I'm in their heads. I'm not a mind-reader, but I do I survey my audience constantly. I make it common practice to gather feedback as well as ask questions through newsletters and social media, and I use that information to speak more clearly to the people I want to reach by echoing the exact words that they spoke to me. That is called *target market research*, and it yields phenomenally valuable information that will make you stand out in the industry because you'll be constantly in a state of refinement and speaking the language of your client.

Although I don't have room in this book to cram in all the marketing tips for using your survey, the ideal-client worksheets will help prepare you to take the next step with your marketing efforts. I want you to work sequentially in growing your business and not hop around wasting time and energy doing things out of order. Just strive to understand your clients for now; don't overwhelm yourself with trying to figure out how to market to them. Collect the data first.

A DEEPER DIVE INTO YOUR IDEAL CLIENT

Why does the person need to hire you?

Why does the person want to hire you?

What is driving the person's desire to hire you? Which emotions are coming into play?

When the client comes to your website, how does that person feel? Desperate, excited, anxious, calm, exhausted, happy? (Take your time here and really consider the deeper needs and thoughts.)

How does the person feel upon seeing your pricing?

How does the person feel while reading your bio page?

How does the person feel while reading your contact page? Welcomed? Pushed away? Confused?

What are the things that the person hopes to get out of the session?

continues on next page

A DEEPER DIVE INTO YOUR IDEAL CLIENT (continued)

What are the things that are significant that the person needs captured, and why are they significant?

If the person had a perfect session from beginning to end, how would it go?

What are the things that turn your client on? What turns that person off?

What are the things that your client values in life, and how does what you do fit in?

What are the problems your client has before hiring you, and how do you solve those problems?

What are the things that keep your client from hiring you?

How do you resolve those issues?

How do you give your clients reasons to talk to you? And about you?

continues on next page

A DEEPER DIVE INTO YOUR IDEAL CLIENT (continued)

What are the negative thoughts that are going through the person's head while looking through your portfolio? (The only way to address these concerns and overcome them is by acknowledging them here. You can do this!)

What does the person worry about?

Why is the person afraid of hiring you? What could go wrong?

How would not being able to hire you make the person feel?

What are the reasons the person couldn't hire you right now?

____

____

____

____

____

What would be the person's dream "Are you freaking kidding me!?" experience that would be worth almost any price? What would that involve? (Details, spill 'em!)

____

____

____

____

____

If that perfect dream session came true, how would the person feel?

____

____

____

____

____

What things in the person's life would change after working with you?
Which parts would improve as a direct result of working with you? ______________

____

____

____

____

____

How to conduct your survey

- Starting a survey is as easy as reaching out to a past client who has the four ideal characteristics and setting up a time to talk. As tempting as it may be to hear customer feedback yourself, however, I highly recommend that someone else—a co-worker, assistant, spouse, friend—perform the survey. Clients generally feel less comfortable being completely honest to the person about whom they are giving feedback. You want clients to be comfortable sharing how they feel as honestly as possible, rather than worrying whether you will be defensive and fire back rebuttals. Even if it means paying someone to conduct the survey, you'll get more valuable information, which will be worth the investment.
- Recording your survey calls and working from a script will also yield better results. For instance, several smartphone apps (including some free options) enable you to record your calls. I like using TapeACall (available for iOS and Android, www.tapeacall.com), because it's easier than note taking and I can listen to the data over and over. In addition, if you record your survey calls, you can easily quote the positive words and phrasing verbatim in your website copy, blog posts, and newsletters to attract like-minded clients who immediately resonate with your past ideal clients. A script will help you organize your thoughts, as well as approach each client consistently.

Script and survey for past clients

tip Don't feel weird about saying "assistant." Anyone assisting you is your assistant. Sound like the professional you want to be!

Whether you survey your highest spending clients, ideal clients, or just clients who you loved working with, try to survey as many as you can. Even if your fledgling business has had only a single client, surveying that one will still give you more data than you had before. Reach out to them with a script something like this:

> Hello, <name>.
>
> I was thinking about you this week and wanted to reach out to you. To refine my business, I am doing some research with past clients who I enjoyed working with. My goal is to better understand your wants and needs so that I can serve you better, as well as attract more amazing clients just like you.
>
> Would you mind allowing my assistant to interview you for 30 minutes to ask about the things you feel are missing in the marketplace when it comes to hiring a photographer, what frustrates you, what you wish photographers were doing better, and a few more questions like that?

If you would be willing to help me out, I'd love to set up a time to have my assistant chat with you.

Would this week be a good time to schedule a call? Thank you so much for your time!

<Your name>

Once you arrange a mutually agreeable time, you can get your research started. The "Survey for Past Ideal Clients" worksheet will give you some ideas what to ask.

Script and survey for potential clients

You can also garner some valuable feedback from potential clients. These are people who you think would be a good fit for your business, not necessarily someone you are actively trying to convince to hire you. Aim to gather only data from the process, not session bookings. Using the sample script that follows and the "Target-Market Client Survey" worksheet, you can better understand what people are thinking, as well as how to determine whether someone is a good fit for you or not.

Hello, <name>,

I have a question for you—actually, I have several, if you would be able to help me out!

Right now, I'm in a process of refining my business practices to better serve my client needs as well as better understand the demands of my marketplace.

Would you mind allowing my assistant to interview you for 30 minutes to ask a few questions about what things are missing in the marketplace when it comes to hiring a photographer, what frustrates you, what you wish photographers were doing better, and the like?

If you would be willing to help me out, I'd love to set up a time to chat with you.

Would this week would be a good time to schedule a call? Thank you so much for your time!

<Your name>

Research is incredibly important for you to understand your clients and what the market can handle. It's not sexy, and it's not fun. But it *is* highly valuable for you not only to know what clients want (and I promise you, they don't just want digital files) but also to understand how they feel. Once you understand how they feel, you can employ your empathy to understand them in all areas so that you can better serve them and better serve your marketplace.

SURVEY FOR PAST IDEAL CLIENTS

How did you come across <*photographer's name*>'s work?

____

____

What was the determining factor that built your trust and confidence that <*photographer's name*> would be a wise investment for you to hire?

____

____

What was the most important thing that you wanted from hiring <*photographer's name*>?

____

____

Did <*photographer's name*> provide all the things that were important to you?

____

____

What qualities does <*photographer's name*> provide that are incredibly important to you?

____

____

Was there any area that exceeded your expectations? If so, what was it?

____

____

What do you emotionally value about photography?

____

____

What is the most important thing to you when hiring a photographer?

____

____

____

____

On a scale of 1 to 5, with 1 being a non-determining factor and 5 a strong determining factor, how important to you is:

- Artistic imagery? 1 2 3 4 5
- Uniqueness? 1 2 3 4 5
- Consistency? 1 2 3 4 5
- Customer service? 1 2 3 4 5
- Attentiveness? 1 2 3 4 5
- The experience of working with the photographer? 1 2 3 4 5
- Having personal involvement in the creative process? 1 2 3 4 5
- Cost? 1 2 3 4 5
- Convenience? 1 2 3 4 5
- Privacy? 1 2 3 4 5
- Luxury experience? 1 2 3 4 5
- Quality of products? 1 2 3 4 5
- Prints? 1 2 3 4 5
- Digitals? 1 2 3 4 5
- Canvases? 1 2 3 4 5
- Albums? 1 2 3 4 5
- Having someone you can return to? 1 2 3 4 5

If you were to tell your friends why <photographer's name> is the best choice for someone to hire, what qualities would you promote and tell others about?

____

____

What were your concerns when you hired <photographer's name>?

____

____

Was there anything that you have struggled with in the past working with other photographers?

____

____

How did <photographer's name> help you in that area that others hadn't?

____

____

TARGET-MARKET CLIENT SURVEY

How do you search for a photographer to hire? Referrals from friends? Google? Another method?

____

____

____

____

What would be a determining factor that builds your trust and confidence that a photographer would be a wise investment for you to hire?

____

____

____

____

What would be the most important thing that you want from hiring a photographer?

____

____

____

____

What qualities do you consider incredibly important to you in a photographer and in working with one?

____

____

____

____

What do you emotionally value about photography?

____

____

____

____

____

On a scale of 1 to 5, with 1 being a nondetermining factor and 5 a strong determining factor, how important to you is each of the following?

- Artistic imagery? 1 2 3 4 5
- Uniqueness? 1 2 3 4 5
- Consistency? 1 2 3 4 5
- Customer service? 1 2 3 4 5
- Attentiveness? 1 2 3 4 5
- The experience of working with the photographer? 1 2 3 4 5
- Having personal involvement in the creative process? 1 2 3 4 5
- Cost? 1 2 3 4 5
- Convenience? 1 2 3 4 5
- Privacy? 1 2 3 4 5
- Luxury experience? 1 2 3 4 5
- Quality of products? 1 2 3 4 5
- Prints? 1 2 3 4 5
- Digitals? 1 2 3 4 5
- Canvases? 1 2 3 4 5
- Albums? 1 2 3 4 5
- Having someone you can return to? 1 2 3 4 5

If you were to tell your friends why <*photographer's name*> is the best choice for someone to hire, what qualities do you generally promote and tell others about?

____

____

____

____

What are your concerns when you hire a photographer?

____

____

____

____

Is there anything that you have struggled with in the past working with other photographers?

____

____

____

____

Your marketplace

You've surveyed your past clients and built a profile of your business soulmate, but there's one important question left to ask: How many ideal clients are in your area? Evaluating your marketplace is as important as identifying and designing your ideal client. You need to be fully aware of what your marketplace can handle and if it is in alignment with the pricing your business needs to set to be profitable and sustainable.

To avoid wasting precious time and valuable resources on a path that leads to a dead end, you must resist the urge to skip doing market research. You must understand not only your income needs and how much your business needs to profit and sustain itself but also what your marketplace and clients need. That's a lot of things to consider when you build your pricing, I know. Taking into account how all the elements work together, however, will help you build a far superior pricing scheme.

It's important to do market research before you start building your price list of all the products you want to offer, because you don't want to price yourself into selling products that your marketplace can't handle. Just because you fall in love with a business idea doesn't mean your marketplace is demanding it, and you don't want to waste energy trying to sell something that no one can afford. For instance, although framing is a phenomenal service to provide, the products you intend to offer may be completely out a client's price point range of affordability. Without market research to tell you this, investing in framing could be a very expensive mistake to learn from because you waste money buying samples as well as selling the products for less than a healthy profit margin.

Research within your local community and with your past clients can reveal, for example, whether your price points are comparable to what others are selling in your marketplace. If someone else is priced similarly, then you know you have competition. Competition is a healthy thing because your clients can make choices based on features and services, instead of the dollar amount. Don't obsess over the numbers research reveals or let them overwhelm or discourage you. Use them as a gauge to know where you land in the marketplace so that you can design your business around where that places you.

How to research your marketplace

The more informed you are about what's being offered by whom in your marketplace, the better you're able to bring a truly unique perspective and set of products to that market. After you've taken a fresh eye at the competition, you'll be in a better place for positioning *your* talents in the world and serving a very specific need that is currently lacking. The "Know Your Competitors" worksheet will help identify and evaluate your closest competitors.

Think hard about the last question of the "Know Your Competitors" worksheet. Maybe your closest competitor takes four months to deliver client galleries for proofing, can be contacted by email only, refuses to travel, meets only in client's homes, or is booked six months in advance. All of these weaknesses are opportunities for you to do better! You don't have to do everything; simply do what your competitor is doing, but do it more effectively: Deliver faster, list your phone number, work on a weekend, travel, take short-notice bookings. Making one tweak at a time to improve your business will help you to stand out. The next worksheet, "Compare and Contrast Yourself with Competitors," will help you critique your business against those in your marketplace.

Making the most of your research

You certainly hope that your research shows you're well-situated in a strong marketplace, but what if it doesn't?

What if you find out that you're the highest-priced studio and that no one else out there is priced in your range? When I had my studio business in Montana, I was the highest-priced photographer in the entire state. Clients also told me that was their determining factor for hiring me. They said it built confidence and trust simply seeing my prices because they knew I had to be a serious businessperson to be able to pull off those prices. They were the type of people who valued someone who was reputable and could deliver high quality in every element. Your marketplace should have its share of these people too.

If you are in an oversaturated community of low-priced photographers, sustaining your business may require your prices to be substantially higher while you provide a high-end luxury experience. Although you may feel more comfortable competing in the mid-range, the high end may be a better bet because no one competing at that price point.

KNOW YOUR COMPETITORS

Whose businesses in your area do you secretly envy?

What makes them incredibly outstanding that you wish you were more like?

Who are your most prominent local competitors?

Competitor 1:

What does the business offer?

____

____

____

What are its price points?

____

____

____

What kind of service does it give?

____

____

____

What is its reputation around town?

____

____

____

What is the business known for?
What is its specialty?

____

____

____

What is your closest competitor doing wrong?

____

____

____

Competitor 2:

What does the business offer?

____

____

____

What are its price points?

____

____

____

What kind of service does it give?

____

____

____

What is its reputation around town?

____

____

____

What is the business known for?
What is its specialty?

____

____

____

What is your closest competitor doing wrong?

____

____

____

Competitor 3:

What does the business offer?

What are its price points?

What kind of service does it give?

What is its reputation around town?

What is the business known for?
What is its specialty?

What is your closest competitor doing wrong?

Competitor 4:

What does the business offer?

What are its price points?

What kind of service does it give?

What is its reputation around town?

What is the business known for?
What is its specialty?

What is your closest competitor doing wrong?

COMPARE AND CONTRAST YOURSELF WITH COMPETITORS

What would make a potential client choose your competitor instead of you?

What do your closest competitors do better than you?

What quality of service do you give? Are you giving your very best, or do you know that you have been cutting corners?

How is your reputation in town?

What do you know that you have been doing wrong in your business but haven't changed?

How are you going to improve on your weaknesses?

What would make a potential client choose you instead of your closest competitors?

What would make a client hire you and only you?

What forms of marketing do your competitors use?

Not everyone out there is shopping for the cheapest price to save money. In fact, when you are growing a business to be profitable and sustainable, you never want to be the cheapest one in town, unless your goal is for high volume and low sales. A better course, and one this book will help you with, is a business model of high sales and low volume. Low volume could be one, five, or ten sessions a week; it's really a matter of how much you are willing to take on.

Shifts you may need to make

Even if you are in your dream market with a perfect business model, you still need to take a measure of reality in account. Specifically, you may have to tweak the volume of clients you bring in and the hours you invest in your business.

Be aware that if you are building a business that requires you to have a price point that is outside the reach of what your area can sustain, you need to revisit that price point that you created in your Chapter 1 worksheets and evaluate where you are going with your business. Don't panic; although the numbers aren't currently working, the business may still be viable. It just means that it may not be viable operating it the way that you want to operate. You may need to adjustment your expectations, ideals, and next actions based on the needs of yourself, your business, your market, and your clients. They need to sync together.

If you are in a struggling financial marketplace, research will help you see ahead of time the shifts you will have to make in your business model—lowering cost of goods, increasing your number of clients, or something else—to keep a lower price point while maintaining profitability.

For instance, suppose you are able to work only ten hours a week, your goal is $2000 per client, and you live in an area with super-low population or surrounded in poverty. That's not a recipe for success; you will have to make some choices. You may need to reconsider the wisdom in starting a business in an area that cannot financially support it. If it's your passion and your life's purpose to have this business, you may need to move or market to a different area and travel. Alternately, you could re-evaluate your model to decrease expenses so that you could bring in more clients at a lower price point while still maintaining a healthy profitable margin. Your budget would have to shift so that you aren't spending as much on overhead and cost of goods, plus you would decrease the amount of time dedicated to each client. In this scenario, however, your marketing efforts will be substantially higher as you will need to bring in more people.

DEMAND DOESN'T GUARANTEE BUYERS

If your marketplace is financially devastated, building a photography business would not be wise even if research seems to indicate a demand for it. Demand does *not* equal profit or sustainability or even guarantee that your product or service will sell. Lots of people demand but are never willing to pay. Make sure that you go into your marketplace fully aware that those demanding will be willing to pay, or you will be footing the bill for that demand.

I learned this lesson the hard way: For years I received tons of requests to create a marketing guide. In 2012, I did a survey asking if anyone would be interested a marketing guide. More than 3000 people responded positively. Encouraged, I released a marketing guide a few weeks after the survey. Demand suggested I should have sold a couple thousand, right? Wrong. I ended up selling only a few hundred copies. Come to find out, no one wanted to pay for marketing advice, even if they demanded it. Everyone wanted it for free.

The most frequent complaint I heard in my follow-up survey was clients wished more free business advice was available. They wanted someone to do the marketing for them, like a done-for-you service. My book did not meet the need that people were willing to pay for, regardless that it met a need that would still solve their problems.

If your community only knows Walmart and every household makes less than $30,000 a year, building an exclusive, luxury business would be unwise. Your business is going to be selling luxury, whether at $25 or $2500. Luxury is an incredibly difficult, or almost impossible, thing to live off of in a struggling marketplace. Even chain studios struggle and go out of business in those areas because selling luxury (even at rock-bottom pricing) is not sustainable.

No matter how your marketplace is doing financially, you are constantly going to have to make choices about which battle you are going to fight because there is never an easy, perfect road.

On the other hand, do not be quick to believe that your community can't support your business. If you live in a town of 10,000 people, statistically speaking 5 percent of that community will still make over $100,000—that's 500 people. Even if you marketed and served only 10 percent of the 500 affluent, which would be 50 people, that's still very possible. So you could have a viable business, even in a small town of 10,000 people. Don't be too hasty with your assumptions of what you can and can't do. This is why market research is vital: It will help you make decisions on facts and not on feelings or assumptions.

3

REVERSE ENGINEERING YOUR PRICING

In this chapter, we put it all together and then go backward. By bringing together your number crunching from Chapter 1 and the research on your ideal client and marketplace from Chapter 2, you can form an end point from which you can reverse engineer your pricing. This is when you'll figure out how you're going to make all of those price points work for your products—from collections to à la carte prints to specialty items. Along the way, you may also realize why your past methods of pricing didn't work out the way you wanted. Let's get started.

Interpret your data your way

While conducting your ideal client surveys or potential client surveys, you're probably gathering some fascinating data about what people want and what they really think. The interesting thing is that not only are people bringing you unique situations, but how you interpret the situations and develop solutions is going to be unique. How you naturally look at a problem and solve it is not necessarily how your competitors would.

Suppose a potential client says, "I wish photographers gave faster turnaround." The solution may be very different to different photographers:

- Joe from PhotoFast Studios may think, "You know, I could do that! I could offer a bonus rush incentive to any client who purchases a collection. I could guarantee delivery within six days versus my usual three-week turnaround for à la carte orders."
- Susan from Shutter Bright may say, "When my clients book their sessions, I will present a very clear and specific time frame so they know when to expect every single step as part of my workflow. If I communicate every step of the way via email updates, they can be confident of progress."
- Austin from inFocus Designs may decide, "That's going to be one of my signature services. Everyone gets their orders hand delivered within four days—no matter who they are or what they get."
- Connie from Prestige Photo may be unimpressed, "What a ridiculous demand! Rushing doesn't fit my brand at all. That's *not* an ideal client for me to focus my business model on. Each step takes a lot of time and energy, and I refuse to rush the process. I'm going to make sure that the clients who hire me know exactly what my turnaround time is so that they are fully aware that I am incredibly attentive to every detail and I refuse to rush and make mistakes. I will assure them that you can't rush a good thing. I'll make sure that they feel secure with that philosophy and that they trust me with the process. This will also eliminate the people who want speed that I can't deliver."

Your own interpretation and your individual solution make you unique. You don't have to do what everyone else is doing. You need to listen and provide solutions based on what the people in the marketplace are saying, not on what other photographers say you "need to do," what they do, or the latest trend. Remember, that trend probably started because one person was successful with the approach because it was unique to her brand.

IT'S ALL IN HOW YOU SAY THE THING

As you gather that data and see the problems and struggles that your market is undergoing, you can learn how to better communicate why your business is unique and not like everyone else. You may discover you don't need to change how you are operating, just how you communicate what you are doing differently.

For example, clients keep telling you that they just want digital files. You can say "Great! I sell digitals. With every set of digital files, I also give complimentary printed proof copies so that you have something tangible. I know how sometimes life gets in the way and you don't get the opportunity to have prints made." Instead of selling to your clients what they don't think they want, you can make the prints sound like a bonus or additional goodie. That's much more effective than telling people who think they want only digital files that you sell only prints. You are meeting their needs and you are giving them even more of what you know they will appreciate. I've never heard of a client annoyed that a photographer gave them too much. It's simply a matter of changing how you present and communicate why you are doing what you are doing.

The same applies to pricing. Interpreting the data you gather expands your point of view from understanding simply what you want to what is wanted by your clients—the ones who are the most important in the reverse engineering scenario because they hold the money. But it's still your unique point of view, so use it to create pricing that benefits both you *and* the ones who are willing to part with their hard-earned money. You must avoid archaic pricing models that don't factor either you or the client into the number-crunching equations.

Avoid archaic pricing models

When starting their businesses, most photographers are lost when it comes to figuring out how to charge for their services and what to offer their clients. So, they turn to other businesses for inspiration and model their pricing after what appears to be working in the marketplace.

Many take their pricing cues from chain photography studios. Unfortunately, that pricing model is archaic and so is the business model behind it. Chain studios are closing their doors left and right, swallowed up by debt or more savvy competitors. That pricing and sales structure was designed to satisfy a model of a high volume of sales at low prices—a model that's not realistic for today's photographer to duplicate on a smaller scale without cutting all corners in quality and customer service. Not to mention that these days, digital cameras are everywhere and Adobe Photoshop is as easy as an app on a smartphone, putting decent, low-cost photos a click away. The way that photography is sold must be changed to be relevant to today's needs.

Another common method of creating a pricing model that fledgling business owners use is to align their session and product fees with what other custom photographers are charging in their marketplaces. Then, they take on as many clients as they possibly can, hoping to make what they need in sales. Some more savvy photographers may do a rough estimation of how many clients they need or how many they want to take on, but few look at their actual hours of availability or factor in the time demands. Although based on more comparable competitors, this is still a poorly built system full of holes that makes troubleshooting difficult when they realize they aren't able to make the profit that they need.

The sale trap

What happens when these flawed models inevitably start to fail? Panic mode sets in. Photographers start to freak out and slash prices to bring in more business. They try sales and discounts to make up the earning loss when their businesses are struggling. This is a sure-fire way to kill a business from ever having hopes of sustainable and consistent profits.

All those "last chance" sales that rarely (if ever) end and deep-discount, direct-mail coupons may get instant sales, but they scream of desperation and generally sleazy business tactics. Studios that use them become known for their "deals," and that's about all anyone goes to them for. Too many sales and discounts hurt your reputation and devalue the investment that your full-paying clients make. When they find out they're paying five to ten times more than your coupon-wielding one-timers, your full-paying, return customers will feel remorse or disappointment—and may not return again.

Although a business can function in that way for a while, it's stressful and completely unpredictable because it lacks a strategy or awareness of the needs of the business. Most find themselves spinning their wheels, constantly trying to figure out how to bring in sales through impulsive sales pitches instead of building a marketing strategy into their methods for long-term results. When a strategy and focused goal are missing, you end up with what I call marketing vomit: selling discounts, sales, special offers, all those gimmicks to get you hired *right now*, so money comes in. There's a better way.

Sell the luxury

Our goal here is to tailor you—your business, your artwork, and your pricing—to be the luxury photographer, because selling photography is a luxury. Think about it. You're selling printed paper, which can't be resold. It doesn't increase in value, you can't promise life-changing benefits, and you can't promise that it can stand the test of time. The elements to selling photography are all purely luxury and satisfy only emotional needs. There are no physical survival needs here. So, whether you consider yourself luxury or not, you are selling luxury, and your pricing and your service need to reflect that as well.

Selling custom photography requires getting away from the archaic pricing models of chain studios and being cheaper than the other guy and instead *thinking* to ensure profitability. You can represent comfort, luxury, and status to the general public. You can create durable, lasting products. You know that durable, luxurious, and lasting products aren't cheap, right? The higher the price point, the more luxurious the treatment and time you can invest without it coming out of your own pocket.

You cannot provide attention to detail and unparalleled customer service if you are scheduled to the brink of insanity and underpriced. Low-volume photographers just don't experience burnout as easily or as quickly as their high-volume counterparts. Low volume (whatever that number means to you) gives you the benefit of time to nurture your creativity, expand your skills in business and your art, serve your clients, and be able to be physically and mentally balanced.

tip Once you establish your pricing, never apologize for it. If you do, clients will lose respect for your work and business. Either you'll be accepted as a luxury photographer or you'll be passed over for the cheap catch of the day. If you want profit and a long-term business, that's a risk you are willing to take, right?

Reverse engineering is the best way

To create a pricing model that gives your clients and your business the attention they both deserve, you need to reverse engineer it. Look at the goal and then work backward. Henry Ford once said, "Whether you think you can or you can't, you are usually right." This is so incredibly true for the reverse engineering process: You must believe in the end point to be able to work yourself backward. If you do, the results will be worth it. I've found that reverse engineering accelerates progress considerably, can give you clear focus when things don't go right, and helps you see the necessary next step to course correct.

Basically, you're going to first create the strategy and then create the pricing to suit the strategy, instead of trying to strategize the other way around. Then you can build your marketing strategy based on the needs of your business and clients, in other words, the needs you identified through your number crunching (Chapter 1, "Getting Started") and research (Chapter 2, "The Ideal Client & Your Marketplace").

Make the big leap

Right now is when many photographers start to doubt the process. The number crunching that you came up with may require your prices to take a huge jump because you were not adequately pricing yourself previously. Let them.

Trust me, it's easier to take one massive leap right now, lose all your clients, and rebuild again for longer-term, returning clients than it is to keep hopping incrementally and still lose the majority with each step up. You're not just losing an instant client with each increase; you're losing a returning client as well. It's a question of longevity: With every price increase, you will need a year to 18 months, assuming you are marketing effectively, to see consistent return on your efforts. Whether you are taking a small leap or a big one, rebuilding will take time. So, make the big leap now and rebuild only once.

PRICING COMES FIRST

No industry establishes its necessary pricing after it has a client base. Pricing always comes first—not free clients or barely paying clients. Those are not a client base; they're test subjects. And test subjects are not clients. You don't build a client base when everyone is getting your work for free. You build a client base from people who have paid your prices.

It's false belief that tells you that you need to keep increasing your prices based on experience and that you have to gradually acclimatize your clients to your pricing instead of just establishing your pricing based on what you need to make.

To get paid what you are worth, you have to charge what you are worth. Charging what you are worth is not a process. It's simply knowing what your numbers are and establishing them. Honor yourself and honor your business, and I promise that you will be rewarded for the efforts.

Stop chasing unicorns

Most people feel that finding clients who are willing to pay them what they are worth is about as likely as finding a unicorn, as if there is a magical magnetism that draws these clients. Sorry, there is no magical process to easing into being paid what you are worth. Just mentally choose what you are going to do and work toward that goal.

tip If you aren't getting hired at all, don't instantly blame your pricing. You might be marketing to the wrong crowd or not accurately communicating what you are selling. Maybe you need to increase the value of what you are selling by offering more attentive customer service, faster turnarounds, or customized experiences.

A cliché like "starving artist" doesn't apply to any other field. Ever hear of starving doctors, starving lawyers, or starving waitresses? They exist, but they miss out on having their own cliché because that's not how people see them. They are all business owners, employees, and entrepreneurs who have high times and hard times financially. But artists, they are just known to starve in their profession. I believe it's self-induced. When you operate your business like an entrepreneur and not like an artist, however, you can break free from the emotional ties of your art determining your profitable worthiness.

You aren't just an artist anymore. If you want to make a livelihood, you have to make this a profession that pays, and that means employing your business brains and wisdom rather than leading with just the heart of an artist.

Your confidence in your skills and your business is reflected in your pricing. If you believe in yourself and your work, your clients will believe in it. Not everyone will be a fit for you, and not everyone is going to be in love with your pricing, whether the price is $50, $500, or $5000. You have to decide that you are okay with that.

What if you don't feel your work is equal to that of Mr. Photography Rockstar, even though your pricing points are similar? Know you *are* worth the money. Why? Because you are a professional. You have calculated and researched. You have done your homework. You know what you are up against. Most importantly, you know wisdom influenced your pricing, not fear. Your decisions based are on data and research.

note The first profitable, paying client is the hardest thing you will ever fight for in your business because what you're really looking for is an act of faith from someone who believes in you. Once you have that first yes, the next yes and all that follow will become progressively easier.

You can't know why or how your competitors chose their pricing, and you don't know what fears they may be having or what their financial profits may be. Don't let the choices of others be your measuring tool for how you should price yourself. Use your research, and with that in mind, it's time for you to start putting that research to work.

Pricing and collections

The first prices you should focus on are for your collections. Pricing collections can be mind-numbing work, especially if you don't have any strategy. But, you do have one: reverse engineering. First, you will establish pricing and then add the products based on what is needed to achieve that price point. To crunch the numbers, you'll use the gross sale per client, session fee, and minimum order requirement (MOR) figures you calculated in the Chapter 1 worksheets.

The pricing method that I teach uses only three collections because I have found that more than three is overwhelming not just to the photographer, who is trying to create them but also to the client, who isn't sure which is the right choice to make. An overwhelmed client sticks with the safest amount with which she feels comfortable because no one wants to choose something and possibly regret it later. Clients rationalize that it's better to buy less than more because they can always come back and get more. But as we know, no one ever comes back to reorder.

Because of this phenomena, I'm a firm believer that less is more, and a big proponent of Barry Schwartz's book, *The Paradox of Choice: Why More Is Less* (Harper Perennial, 2005). It argues that eliminating consumer choices can greatly reduce or eliminate anxiety for shoppers. Schwartz explains it:

> "When people have no choice, life is almost unbearable. As the number of available choices increases, as it has in our consumer culture, the autonomy, control, and liberation this variety brings are powerful and positive. But as the number of choices keeps growing, negative aspects of having a multitude of options begins to appear. As the number of choices grows further, the negatives escalate until we become overloaded. At this point, choice no longer liberates, but debilitates. It might even be said to tyrannize.... Our evaluation of our choices is profoundly affected by what we compare them with, including comparison with alternatives that exist only in our imaginations. The same experience can have both delightful and disappointing aspects. Which of these we focus on may determine whether we judge the experience to be satisfactory or not."

How your client feels about the ordering process has a huge impact in not only your profiting from the sale but also in sustaining him as a returning client. If the plethora of collection choices leaves him stressed, overwhelmed, or anxious about the ordering process, you can guarantee that he isn't going to be excited to do it again. Your clients will dread that experience, even if they love your photography.

In her book, *The Art of Choosing* (Twelve, 2011). Sheena Iyengar writes

> "...when people are given a moderate number of options (like 4 to 6) rather than a large number (20 to 30), they are more likely to make a choice, are more confident in their decisions, and are happier with what they choose.... Your enjoyment of the chosen options will be diminished by your regret over what you had to give up. In fact, the sum total of the regret over all the 'lost' options may end up being greater than your joy over your chosen options, leaving you less satisfied than you would have been if you had had less choice to begin with."

Following Iyengar's advice of offering a limited number of choices, I always stick with just three collections. Any more are completely unnecessary and will just overwhelm. Likewise, fewer than three collections would not be helpful either because then clients would be faced with the most overwhelming option of all: the à la carte menu. The packaged choices are what help clients narrow down all the thoughts swirling in their heads and nudge them to a decision. You don't have to be a pushy salesperson to nudge them; all you have to do is show them and let the benefits speak for themselves.

The psychology of collections

My strategy is to start your collections at a price point that is just above the minimum order requirement you calculated in Chapter 1. The advantage to this approach is that you can leverage each sale without having to be pushy about it and give your clients an opportunity to spend more if they want more.

When you present collections without a minimum order requirement, a client may feel like she has to buy the base-level collection, even if it's six times more costly than the mental budget she brought to the sales session. Few clients want to look like total cheapies, spending $200 when collections start at $1200. But when confronted with the pricing for the first time in the sales session, they are suddenly dealing with sticker shock while trying to come to terms with exceeding their price points of affordability because they love their images and don't want to offend the photographer. In the urgency of the moment they may feel pushed into spending more than they can afford and suffer buyer's remorse.

When you clearly state your MOR but offer no collections, the outcome is no better. If clients come in with the knowledge that they have to spend only your stated MOR, say $500, and you simply offer à la carte options, you'll find that their sales will hover around that $500 requirement and rarely go over it.

Instead, clearly state a minimum order requirement up front, say $900, and offer collections starting a bit above that, say $1125. Suddenly, your client feels like she is free to choose how much she can spend. She already mentally spent that MOR before hiring you, so she will be less focused on that figure in the sales session because she is no longer in sticker-shock mode. She's already been processing that number for a couple weeks now, maybe even months. The longer you keep thinking about a number, the easier it is to get comfortable with the idea of it. When you present the collections, she starts seeing how much *more* bang for her buck she can get if she spends over the minimum. She will be less overwhelmed by the options because now they are on *her* terms.

You specified your terms, which was the minimum order requirement, and your clients agreed. Now the final sale is on their terms. They still have the choice to spend the minimum, which I consider an emotional safety net for them or to spend more only an increment more for a collection.

note If you haven't already calculated your session fee and minimum order requirement in Chapter 1's "Your Numbers Bible" worksheet, I recommend doing so before continuing.

Calculate the price points

Now that you're clear on why reverse engineering three collection prices from your minimum order requirement is a good idea, it's time to whip out your calculator and figure out those three price points.

If you are not yet established as a photographer, price your three collections at 25 percent, 50 percent, and 75 percent higher than your MOR. If you are more established and you don't foresee any additional price increases for a few years, then I recommend pricing collections at 25 percent, 75 percent, and 125 percent higher than your MOR.

tip To determine a percentage, simply divide the desired percentage by 100 to convert it to a decimal and then multiply it by the MOR.

For instance, assuming an MOR of $500, a new business would charge $625 (500 + [500 × .25]), $750 (500 + [500 × .50]), and $875 (500 + [500 × .75]) and an established business's collections would price out at $625, $875, and $1125. The "Collection Price-Point Calculations" worksheet will help you organize your numbers.

Collections as rewards

Are you freaking out over those "high" numbers on your worksheet? Don't. Instead, consider this: Collections are rewards for well-paying clients. Collections are *not* a way to offer a ton of stuff for a ridiculously low price. Forget that archaic pricing model, and look to your future full of repeat clients.

COLLECTION PRICE-POINT CALCULATIONS

Session Fee: ____

Minimum Order Requirement (MOR): ______________________________

Phase 1: Collection Prices for Non-established Photographers

Recommended percentage increases: 25%, 50%, 75%

______(.25 x MOR) + ______(MOR) =_________(price of smallest collection)

______(.50 x MOR) + ______(MOR) =_________(price of midrange collection)

______(.75 x MOR) + ______(MOR) =_________(price of largest collection)

Phase 2: Collection Prices for Established Businesses

Recommended percentage increases: 25%, 75%, 125%

______(.25 x MOR) + ______(MOR) =________(price of smallest collection)

______(.75 x MOR) + ______(MOR) =________(price of midrange collection)

______(1.25 x MOR) + _____(MOR) =________(price of largest collection)

Collection Price Range:

Collection 1 (smallest): ______________________________________

____

____

____

Collection 2 (midrange): ______________________________________

____

____

____

Collection 3 (largest): _______________________________________

____

____

____

The purpose of collections is to give rewards and incentives for purchasing *beyond* the minimum order requirement. Your client still can buy whatever she wants off the à la carte pricing, and she only has to spend that minimum. Buying a collection is not a requirement, and your clients should feel no pressure to buy one. It's completely their choice; all you require is that MOR.

If they want to get more bang for their buck, however, you will give them incentives—rewards built into the collection because they are buying more than just the minimum. That is the strategy behind collections for maximizing sales: natural upselling without you having to be a pushy salesman. Clients will see the value for themselves and determine whether it's worth spending a little extra to get a whole lot more. Because clients perceive the choice as their own, not something that they are pushed into, quite often they *will* spend that little extra.

When your collections are built strategically, you can expect to see about 10 percent of clients buying your largest package, 10 percent buying your smallest, and 80 percent buying your middle. It's a good example of the 80/20 rule at work. (Also called the Pareto principle, the rule states that for many events, roughly 80 percent of the effects come from 20 percent of the causes.) Most of the world likes the middle choice; it's comfortable there—not too cheap and not too extravagant.

We'll be doing more with these collections in Chapter 4, "The Grand Reveal," when we add all the goodies to them. For now, however, just focus on establishing your collection price points and whether you want to grow into your pricing with the Phase 1 collections or whether you are in Phase 2 and you want to settle into your pricing longer term.

Pricing à la carte and specialty items

With your three collection sizes priced, let's continue reversing to price your gift prints, à la carte prints, digital files, and specialty items, such as canvas prints and albums. If your clients are spending only the minimum order requirement, the à la carte prices are the ones they will pay. Because you need to discount the à la carte prices for your collections but continue to make a healthy profit margin, you need to position these at a higher level; à la carte and specialty item pricing is premium pricing, but we're not simply over-inflating prices to drive clients to collections. Instead, we'll start your price sheet with what clients will think of as a bonus: the gift print price.

Pricing gift prints

Your price for gift prints, those extra 10x13 and smaller prints that clients need for family and friends, will form the basis of all your à la carte and specialty product prices. And the best thing is, no matter how many gift print sizes you intend to offer, you need to decide on only *one* price.

One price fits all may sound like a radical concept, but think for a minute. You invest the same amount of time and energy in a photograph, whether it is printed at 5x7 or 8x10. Why charge less for a print that is just 3 inches smaller? You wouldn't want to buy an ill-fitting size-small shirt because the size medium cost too much more, yet that's the sort of decision we force on our clients when we price prints by size.

Before I changed to offering gift prints at a single price, my clients tended to buy the smallest size because it was cheaper. Now I present the single price for a gift print of any size (10x13, 8x10, 5x7, 4x6, or a set of wallets), and a magical thing has happened. My sales for those 4x6s and 5x7s have become almost non-existent. Everyone wants that 8x10. It is easier for me to sell because clients almost always choose bigger over smaller if it's for the same price. The single price makes the decision easier for clients as well, meaning they're more relaxed with the process and likely to think more highly of you and your business. Clients love being able to pick what they want.

It's your turn to pick now. Take a look at **Table 3.1**, which is a super simple cheat sheet to help you price your specialty items. You don't have to do any number crunching at all; just consult the row for your MOR and session fee and then slide left to find the appropriate price for each type of specialty item. For example, a minimum order requirement of $1200 corresponds to a session fee in the $151 to $250 range and a gift print price of $45 to $50 per print.

note If you haven't already calculated your session fee and minimum order requirement in Chapter 1's "Your Numbers Bible" worksheet, I recommend doing so now.

Table 3.1 Gift Print and Specialty Pricing Chart

MOR/SALES GOAL	SESSION FEE	GIFT PRINT	DIGITAL FILE	SPECIALTY ITEMS MARKUP
$0–$300	$100	$30	$90	(do not sell)
$300– $1000	$101–$150	$40	$120	(do not sell)
$1000–$1500	$151–$250	$45–$55	$135–$165	5× cost of goods
$1500–$3000	$250–$350	$55–$75	$165–$225	5.5×–6.5× cost of goods
$3000–$9000+	$350–$550	$75+	$225+	7× cost of goods

THE BOTTOM LINE

Only a small percentage of businesses consistently achieve sales of more than $3000. If your numbers are bringing you into this pricing category (the bottom row in Table 3.1), understand that you will have to be doing a lot of marketing and offer amazing customer service. Your brand needs to focus on luxury while you deliver high value and quality. This category is not impossible, but it does require a high level of structure and strategizing from start to finish to cater a superior client experience.

note I don't believe in the psychology of numbers and am tired of the marketing trick of ending prices in 4, 7, or 9. I mentally round those up, like I suspect most people do. To save my clients the trouble and make their calculations easier, I round my prices to multiples of 5. But that's just me; pick the numbers you prefer for yours.

Circle the appropriate gift print price or price range for your MOR now; you'll need this number shortly to determine the rest of your à la carte and specialty prices.

Because all the à la carte pricing for wall prints, as well as specialty item prices, are related to the gift print prices, all the numbers in this chart (and your overall price sheet) flow together and have consistency. Consistency is what determines that your pricing makes sense to your clients. It's easier for them to trust that you know what you are doing when everything is consistent. Trust and confidence gets shaky when the numbers look thrown together without a consistent strategy in place. Think of it this way: You're in a store selling handbags all priced in the $200 to $400 range—except one marked $15. You're going to wonder what is wrong with that bag because its price is inconsistent with the rest. Table 3.1 takes away that big question mark by providing consistency across your range of products.

It's important to me that you understand the reasoning behind the method so that you'll have confidence in the pricing information and understand what it is accomplishing. To that end, take a closer look at the next column of the chart.

Pricing digital files

Mention digital files to a group of photographers, and you're sure to hear a range of opinions. I am pretty much smack dab in the middle of the debate's spectrum: I don't believe that selling digital files alone is a wise business move, but I don't believe eliminating them completely is wise either.

If you build a model based solely on digital files, you could end up losing your sustainability. The drawback to digital files is that although clients want them, they often end up languishing unprinted on hard drives. If a client isn't actively using his investment, if it serves very little purpose, he'll have a hard time buying that luxury more than once. Communicating features and benefits is also harder when you are selling just digital files. You lose a huge opportunity to get your clients attached not only to their images but also to working with you because of the value that you add to their life and their emotional needs.

Among those who sell digital files, the most successful photographers I know also sell tangible products. A digital-only business is too new concept in the industry for there to be much proof yet that it can sustain itself, so I am very cautious.

At the same time, if clients are willing to pay for digital files, don't ignore this low-hanging fruit because you feel like it goes against your artistic integrity. It's a business decision. Get over the fact that your client will print at inferior print labs, or she may decimate your beautiful work by converting it to grayscale for a quick black-and-white print. You cannot sustain a business that is more focused on doing everything your way with no regard to what the clients want and value. If you want to build a profitable business, your clients matter more than artistic integrity. (Besides, 10 years from now your skills will have matured so much that you will cringe at what you are creating now.) So just go where the money is, and right now, the money is in digital files.

My method for pricing digital files is to set their per-file price at a minimum of three times the cost of a gift print. At this level, they are profitable and will be seen as valuable, and they won't devalue the gift prints. I have also found that pricing digital files double the gift print cost looks less strategic to clients, as if you just guessed at a number. Some photographers price four to five times higher than gift prints, but after experimenting I think that three times is much more effective overall. Consult the fourth column of Table 3.1 for suggestions of some specific numbers, and circle those associated with your MOR and session fee.

note If you're wondering about selling digital files in packages, hold that thought. I'll discuss that in Chapter 4 when we build your collections.

If a client questions the higher price for digital files over gift prints, simply explain that it's cheaper for him to purchase a digital file and print it multiple times than to purchase the same number of gift prints. Besides saving him money in the long run, he can potentially print enlargements from it as well. The goal is to shift the client's mind-set to what he can do with the digital file that makes it more valuable.

Pricing for wall prints

Tip To determine a percentage, simply divide the desired percentage by 100 to convert it to a decimal and then multiply it by the gift print price.

The value of a stunning photograph displayed proudly on the wall, on the other hand, will be obvious to most clients, and no à la carte price list is complete without a listing of wall-sized prints. **Table 3.2** makes filling in the numbers super-duper easy. All you have to do is select the appropriate column for your gift print, and then you'll find your entire price list written out below it. Again, these wall print prices are based on percentages of your established gift print price. If your exact gift print price is not listed in the chart, you can calculate it easily with the increase percentages listed for each print size. For instance, if you sell gift prints for $37, a 16x20 wall print would be 250 percent of that price or $92.50 (37 × 2.50).

Although the prices in Table 3.2 are based on your gift print prices, you need to keep one other factor in mind: cost of goods. A ton of variables go into creating a product—your packaging, materials, equipment, overhead, cost of outsourcing oversized prints—and all are constantly shifting. To ensure your print prices allow for a margin of profitability, your cost of goods for a print should be no more than 15 percent of its sale price. If you're investing more than $15 to create a print you're selling for $100, for instance, it's time to make adjustments to materials, methods, or price.

These price points cover almost every popular printing lab online that I looked into. They all are pretty much close to being the same, maybe a few dollars difference here and there, but still all generally priced the same. If you are keeping a close eye on your budget, you'll be able to tell whether something is out of whack and what needs to be changed.

Table 3.2 Wall Print Cheat Sheet

GIFT PRINT	$30	$35	$40	$45	$50	$55	$60	$65	$70	$75	$80
11x14/11x16 (150%)	$45	$52.50	$60	$67.50	$75	$82.50	$90	$97.50	$105	$112.50	$120
16x20/16x24 (250%)	$75	$87.50	$100	$112.50	$125	$137.50	$150	$162.50	$175	$187.50	$200
20x24/20x30 (400%)	$120	$140	$160	$180	$200	$220	$240	$260	$280	$300	$320
24x36/24x30 (650%)	$195	$227.50	$260	$292.50	$325	$357.50	$390	$422.50	$455	$487.50	$520
30x40 (800%)	$240	$280	$320	$360	$400	$440	$480	$520	$560	$600	$640
40x60 (950%)	$285	$332.50	$380	$427.50	$475	$522.50	$570	$617.50	$665	$712.50	$760

COST OF GOODS AND BUDGET TRACKING

As you remember from Chapter 1, your cost of goods sold, or *COGS*, is the total breakdown of one-time expenses (packaging, printing, and so on) required to create a product. You will always be able to total up what it costs to produce an item when you know the cost of goods. The trouble is that there is no easy way to make sure that you are consistently pricing yourself so that you have the exact numbers of expenses all taken into account.

The best method that you can implement to ensure that you are priced accurately is budget tracking. By paying close attention to the numbers you will be able to monitor if you are overspending in any budgeted category. Ask your bookkeeper to create a budget for you using your pricing percentages and then track to make sure that you are sticking to it. Printing (and reviewing) weekly, semimonthly, or monthly reports can help you make sure that you are on track with spending and earning.

Make sure that you stay within your pricing percentages and adjust accordingly. If your cost of goods rises above the acceptable percentage (15 percent of the sale price), you will need to cut back either what you are spending or cut back in another category.

Pricing for canvas prints

Fine-art prints, such as canvases, offer clients an extra touch of luxury. Luxury, however, comes at a price, and **Table 3.3** offers some suggestions. If you sell metal, velvet, watercolor, or other specialty prints instead of canvases, their prices would fit the prices and markup factors listed in Table 3.3 as well. Again, the suggested prices are designed to be consistent with various price points for gift prints, so consult the appropriate column.

I based these cheat sheet prices on a rough cost of goods estimate that used ProDPI (www.prodpi.com) for the actual printing. I then multiplied that number by the appropriate markup factor for each gift print category and rounded the result to the nearest $25.

If you want more specific numbers, total up your cost of goods (including the rate your printing lab charges) and multiply it by the appropriate cost of goods markup factor. Finally, double-check that your cost of goods is less than 15 percent of your final price and that the price is consistent with the rest of the numbers on your price sheet. Remember, you don't want to sell a $2000 product when everything else is under $100, and you don't want to sell a $25 product when everything is over $200. Watch those numbers and make sure that everything feels like it makes sense.

tip If you can't price something by marking it up five times the cost of goods, it doesn't belong on your price list.

Table 3.3 Canvas Cheat Sheet

GIFT PRINT PRICE	$50	$60	$70	$75	$80
COGS Markup Factor	5×	5.5×	6×	6.5×	7×
11X14/11X16	$325	$350	$400	$425	$450
16X20/16X24	$525	$575	$625	$675	$750
20X24	$600	$650	$700	$750	$825
20X30	$700	$775	$850	$925	$1000
24X30	$750	$825	$900	$975	$1050
24X36	$850	$950	$1025	$1125	$1200
30X40	$1075	$1200	$1300	$1400	$1525

WHEN NOT TO SELL CANVASES AND ALBUMS

Although canvas prints and albums can bring a touch of distinction to your product list, they also bring a case of sticker shock to your budget. Canvases and albums both have a high cost of goods. To make a decent profit margin, therefore, you need to mark them up a minimum of five times that cost. For some studios this just won't make sense. If your minimum required order is less than $1000 and your gift print price is below $50, for example, I suggest you don't sell canvases or albums. At a markup of five times the COGS, their price point would be *far* out of the range of what a client shopping for a sale under $1000 could afford.

Albums are the worst culprits. You'll either spend several hours to design them or pay to outsource them, which is often the better choice. Factoring in an outsourced layout, your total cost of goods will be in the neighborhood of $300 for a good-quality album. That may not sound like much, but if your average sale is about $500, there is no way that you are going to sell albums at the minimum five-times markup price of $2500.

True, a lot of photographers do sell albums for only a two- or three-times markup. The problem with this strategy is you are basically paying for a client to buy the product because the profit margin is super low—so low that it will barely cover the time you invest (think of your hourly value) as well as cost of goods. Instead of pieces of distinction, albums can turn into distraction pieces; a client spends more money to give you less of a profit, instead of buying something that would give you a better profit. It's better to not even offer albums and canvases until you are able to price and sell them at appropriate price points; otherwise, you'll kill all your other sales.

Pricing for albums

When it comes to luxury photography, nothing will set you apart more from the shoot-and-burn photographer and lower-priced point studios than a session album. A session album is either a hard- or soft-covered book that features your session images printed directly onto the pages. These are not books with slip-in sleeves for inserting prints. You (or someone you hire) create a layout design, and then you send it away to be created. Some have sturdy 2mm-thick pages and lush leather bindings, such as the options available from KISS Books (http://kiss.us), White House Custom Color (www.whcc.com), or Finao (www.finaoonline.com). Others, such as those from Artifact Uprising (www.artifactuprising.com), are more like coffee table books with a hard cover and magazine-style pages.

tip Before you spend money buying lots of studio samples to show your clients, buy actual albums in a couple styles for yourself. Even if you're not totally happy with a design, it won't be a waste of money because at least your own pictures will be showcased. After you know that you love a particular album, then get a studio sample.

Each style has advantages, so my advice is to find an album that you love and stick with it. Make it your signature album, one that is recognized when someone sees it on a friend's shelf. If the client's friend loves it, she is going to want one, and want the same one. When you are constantly changing album companies, your clients can feel cheated if they already fell in love with one style and now you are offering another. Likewise, how you design your signature album is part of your branding, a way that you consistently provide the same look, feel, and emotion in everything that you present to your clients.

When I had my studio, I found providing a standard-sized album of 30 pages was the easiest way to ensure consistent pricing. I made it a habit to not overshoot because I found that the more images I presented, the more overwhelmed the client was. If I had a really strong session that provided more than 30 images, I saved those to add for filler to the album, thereby surprising the client with bonus images they didn't expect. I didn't add pages; rather, some pages would have two to three images each.

tip Albums can be excellent money makers but can easily turn into time drains equally easily. Outsourcing album designing is one of those expenses that is totally worth the price. If you just can't let go of the control, however, Khara Plicanic's Album Moxie (Peachpit, 2013) offers designs and strategies for working more efficiently.

To be consistent, my price, as always, was tied to the price of my gift print. To be profitable, it was based on my cost of goods to produce the album (outsourcing design, printing, and packaging). **Table 3.4** lists the appropriate markup factors for each level of gift print pricing. For example, if your gift print is $50, you'll mark up your albums at five times their COGS; if they're $70, you'll mark up six times their COGS; and so on. (If your gift prints sell for less than $50, see the sidebar "When Not to Sell Canvases and Albums.")

Table 3.4 Album Formula Cheat Sheet

Gift Print Price	$50	$60	$70	$75	$80
Markup to COGS	5×	5.5×	6×	6.5×	7×

SELL THE SESSION

The wonderful thing about albums is that they are a fantastic way to sell all the session images without having to hand over the digital files. All of the client's favorite images are organized in a story-telling manner, which gives greater impact to the entire session and an emotional connection when the imagery is put together.

If you are a details-type photographer, albums are an absolute must because they provide a home for those creativity-pushing, detail-element images that you absolutely love but most of the time clients don't purchase. While those images looked gorgeous on your blog or in a magazine spread and clients may totally swoon, rarely are the shots profitable for a sale. You want to find a way to sell those images as they enhance the rest of the session, so the session album is where you pull it all together.

If you have signature shots, they may not be strong for sales on their own, but they reflect your branding and who you are. Albums offer a way that you can provide them to your client and become "known" for a certain look in your work.

Compile your price sheet

To create your final à la carte price list, fill in the "Your à la Carte Price Sheet" worksheet with the numbers you calculated in this chapter. Remember that these numbers were designed to carry your business for some time. Constantly changing à la carte prices can make a business appear flakey or uncertain, so change them only when you are ready to make significant changes in your business. Before you change your à la carte pricing, consider tweaking and testing your collections instead to make sure that you are maximizing your sales. You'll learn more about filling and tweaking collections in the next chapter.

YOUR À LA CARTE PRICE SHEET

Session Fee: ______________________________

Minimum Order Requirement: ______________________________

Digital Files (price per file): ______________________________

Gift Prints: ______________________________

Wall Prints:

11x14/11x16 ______________________________

16x20/16x24 ______________________________

20x24/20x30 ______________________________

24x36/24x30 ______________________________

30x40 ______________________________

40x60 ______________________________

10x20 ______________________________

Canvases (if offering)

(sizes) ______________________________

____

____

Session Album (if offering; limit to no more than three sizes and cover options)

(sizes) ______________________________

____

____

Additional Specialty Products (press printed cards, etc.)

____

____

____

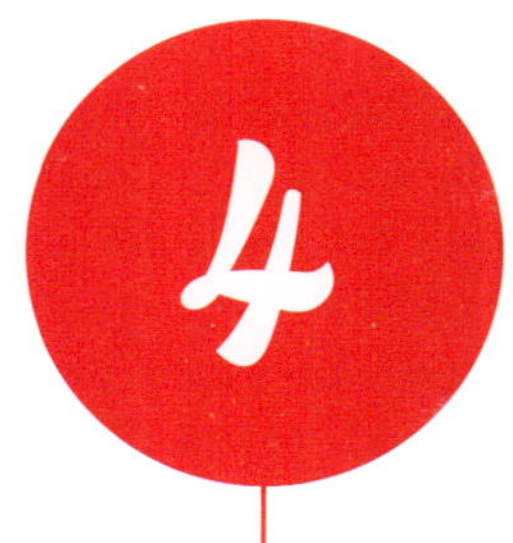

THE GRAND REVEAL

Whenever you learn something in business, it opens up another pathway to learn something else. Learning pricing strategies in Chapter 3 opened new questions: What do you put in those newly priced collections? How do you effectively communicate your price list and collections' benefits to your clients? What's the role of website copy? Should you focus on online or in-person sales? This chapter has the answers you're waiting for—all the details so that you can fill out your collections and present your pricing to your clients and marketplace.

Yes, these answers will probably open more pathways and questions, but I want to create in you a hunger for more. If you dig deeper, you'll gain a better understanding of how to grow and prosper in your business. We'll start the journey with some strategies for filling your collections and then move on to selling their benefits.

Build tweakable collections

Compared to the number crunching and research, collection building is one of the easiest aspects of the whole pricing process, but it is not a one-and-done task. Finding the perfect combination of products will require some tweaking even after you start presenting the collections to your clients. Because you established price points first, you'll be changing only the contents, not the cost. Your returning clients won't freak out when you make these changes; few memorize exact product groupings, but most remember prices, specifically your session fee, minimum order requirement, and gift print cost.

By establishing your price points first and then tweaking the content of your collections, you gain greater flexibility to test what will sell best and what your clients will be the most drawn to, as well as on how to present it. You don't want to be stuck in that box where you encounter problems with your collections and then either live with them or start all over from scratch to fix them.

Test what works

I'll be honest: I can't tell you the perfect mixture of products to put in your collections. What works and what doesn't ultimately relies on the wants and needs of your unique marketplace, how you present and sell, and your style of imagery. For instance, do your images sell better as collections of smaller prints or do they sell better as larger images? I don't know all the answers, and you may not even know them—but that's okay!

note Remember, your marketplace cannot tell you where to set your price points; only you can determine that by factoring your goals, time, and expenses. If you let clients tell you, you'll run yourself into the ground. Face it, everyone prefers lower prices when asked.

Research and observation hold the key. Test various product groupings, and pay close attention to what people are buying. If things aren't working, do another client survey. You can always rely on client surveys to help you refine what you are doing in your business. Only your clients know what they want, no one else. When in doubt, research, and make performing surveys a regular practice in your business. Whenever you're having a hard time understanding your clients or the marketplace, ask questions directly of those people to find the answers. Assumptions are a dangerous thing to build a business on.

Add digital files strategically

Everyone wants digital files, as I'm sure your client surveys are telling you, and digital-only collections (without any prints) are becoming very popular. Digital files also are incredibly beneficial for factoring value into a collection without raising its cost of goods. If you want to add more value to a collection while reducing the overall cost of goods, add digital files.

My method of using digital files strategically is to sell them as elements within the print collections, as well as to offer an all-inclusive digital file option (which comes with a set of proofs) on the à la carte menu, setting it apart from the actual collections. That way if someone truly only wants all the digital files and nothing else, he can just buy that. By including them in print collections, I ensure clients can still get their hands on their favorites shots as digital files, even if they don't get them all.

tip Don't make digital files the basis for your business. Although clients say they want digital files, I've found they're not always willing to pay for them. Watch your surveys carefully to determine what your clients say they value and how that affects their spending habits.

Pricing an all-inclusive collection of digital files is easy, because you already determined your price for a single file in Chapter 3. Simply multiply that price by 10, and there's your price for all-inclusive collection of digital files plus a tangible, deliverable set of proofs. Although some photographers offer 5×7 proofs, I usually provide my proofs as 4×6 prints because that size slips into albums easily.

The price of this digital-and-proof collection will always be slightly more than your minimum order requirement. Clients can choose to buy the minimum in digital files *or* spend a little bit more and get the whole session. The best part is that no matter which choice your client goes with, you will *always* make a profit and your cost of goods will *always* be under that 15 percent.

By now, you've done your math (for instance, 3 × $40 per gift print = $120 per digital file; $120 × 10 = $1200 as the all-inclusive price), and you may be wondering if your digital file price point is too high. Remember the psychologically behind sales: The more someone spends for something, the more they value it—digital files included. The more clients pay, the more urgency that they will feel to actually print and do something with the files because they've invested a substantial amount. So essentially, by charging these higher rates for digital files, you are building in more opportunity for overall satisfaction because clients are more likely to use them. Sell them on the cheap, and clients won't feel the value as much, may never print or use the files, and will be less satisfied overall because their money didn't produce a result for the investment. Clients will turn that lack of satisfaction against you and probably won't return; they just can't justify doing it again because they didn't follow through on their end.

DON'T DANGLE BAIT, PROVIDE VALUE

A common (and big) mistake that photographers make with their pricing is to price their collections at lower price points than the actual sales that they must make to be profitable and sustainable if every client bought that smallest collection. Although these bargain-price, base-level collections sell, the photographers feel resentful that their clients don't order enough or order the biggest package.

Like those chain studios dangling the bait of $6 or $12 print packages for a single pose, these photographers are hoping the lure of low prices will entice clients to the studio where they will want to buy more poses at the photographer's higher à la carte pricing. If the ploy doesn't work, the photographer feels resentful. If it does work, clients often feel they've been pressured (or tricked) into overspending—not what we want to do to build fierce client loyalty in a luxury market.

If you can't be happy with someone buying it, then don't sell it. Because you calculate your minimum order requirement, you know the lowest amount that you are willing to make to be satisfied. Using your minimum order requirement (MOR), you positioned your collections prices *above* that minimum so that you could better leverage your sales for greater profitability. You can't feel good about your business when you are constantly slashing prices, giving discounts, and not getting paid what you need to maintain operation expenses.

Collections should make both *you* and your clients happy. Focus on filling them with value, not playing pricing mind games.

tip Never sell low-resolution or watermarked files. Clients don't understand resolution differences and won't bother to learn, but they will be disappointed with the horrific results of printing a low-resolution image. Don't sell disappointment; sell only full resolution. Save watermarked files for social media sharing or online proofing because they literally have no value.

After I started selling my digital files for $250, my clients began asking me tons of questions about the best places to order the highest-quality prints. They wanted to make sure they were making the best choice for their investments and to take action as soon as possible. I saw a totally different attitude, and it really helped me justify the price of selling the digitals.

Create stacking collections

Don't make the common mistake of building one collection of all prints, another that's all digital, and a third that mixes a ton of things. This approach leaves clients overwhelmed with no basis for comparing the value of their choices. The result is usually that clients retreat to buying only the minimum from your à la carte menu.

Instead, make your collections easy to understand so that clients can easily see their value and decide spending more than the minimum is worthwhile. Clients appreciate clear, comparable choices, such as basic, premium, and deluxe options.

One way to ensure this is to create collections with contents that stack like building blocks on top of each other. Collection 1, the lowest-cost option, serves as your base. Collection 2 then contains everything in Collection 1, plus a little more, and finally Collection 3, the highest option, contains everything in Collection 2, plus even more. The three choices build on each other; they don't compete with each other.

To demonstrate the stackable approach and the behind-the-scenes decisions that go into building collections, the next few sections will walk you through several examples. For simplicity, I've arranged the collections into three groups: collections without specialty items, those with specialty items, and digital collections.

Example collections without specialty items

Shown in the sidebar "Collections Without Specialty Items," the first group of example collections is designed for photographers who aren't offering specialty items yet. It assumes an MOR of $750, gift print price of $40, and digital file price of $120 per file. The collection price points correspond to the percentage increases (25 percent, 50 percent, and 75 percent) recommended for new businesses in Chapter 3, "Reverse Engineering Your Pricing." (You'll notice I rounded to the nearest $50 for easier calculations.) For this pricing group, you won't yet be selling canvases or albums, so prints and digital files are your friend.

note See Chapter 3 for advice on when to add specialty items to your collections.

You'll notice all three collections list a quantity of gift prints first. Gift prints are an excellent base for your collections because their cost of goods is low and they are always popular. Clients love them because off-the-shelf frames are easy to find and no custom framing is needed. When you have a simple collection structure, adding or removing a couple gift prints makes tweaking easy, as well.

All three collections also offer clients the freedom of choice. Clients can choose their preference of gift print and wall print sizes. Choice is a great way to get your clients to feel even more excited about the process, while simplifying your sales sessions. If your client wants a wall gallery, for instance, you can point him to a collection and then help him design his own gallery by choosing the wall print sizes that would work best for him. Listing the largest option (20×30 for wall prints and 10×13 for gift prints) encourages clients to go big. Clients focus on which size they want rather than which size is the cheapest. I used 20×30 as the largest wall print option, but you can tweak that size, depending on whether you want to sell bigger or smaller—and client feedback, of course.

COLLECTIONS WITHOUT SPECIALTY ITEMS

$750 MOR, gift print $40, digital file $120

Collection 1, $950 (à la carte value of $1440)

- 8 gift prints (10×13 or smaller)
- 4 wall prints (20×30 or smaller)
- 4 digital files
- 10 percent off additional à la carte products

Collection 2, $1150 (à la carte value of $2160)

- 12 gift prints (10×13 or smaller)
- 6 wall prints (20×30 or smaller)
- 6 digital files
- 20 percent off additional à la carte products

Collection 3, $1350 (à la carte value of $3120)

- 16 gift prints
- 8 wall prints (20×30 or smaller)
- All-inclusive digital files (plus set of 4×6 proofs)
- 50 percent off additional à la carte products

Digital files increase the value of each collection, while decreasing the overall cost of goods of each. Remember, your all-inclusive digital file package is worth ten digital files. Working backward from Collection 3, which contains the all-inclusive set, Collections 2 and 1 should each contain proportionally fewer. For the example, I included six digital files in Collection 1 and four in Collection 2.

When tweaking print sizes and numbers of items, be sure to keep your cost of goods below 15 percent of the collection's price point to ensure it's profitable. If your cost of goods rises above 15 percent, you can simply lower the number of wall prints you have in a collection and increase the number of digital files to give additional value. Collections are super easy to tweak as you go; simply pay attention to how your sales are doing and if you are staying within your budgeted percentages.

The cost of goods is for your benefit, but the comparable à la carte value is for the client's. When you present your collections, always show your clients not only the collections' prices but also the comparable à la carte value for their contents, such as Collection 1, $950 (à la carte value $1440). When totaling up the value of a collection, simply add up the individual à la carte prices. For the wall prints, use the price of the largest size clients can choose. For instance, for Collection 1, I added $320 (eight gift prints at $40 each), $640 (four 20×30 wall prints at $160 each), and $480 (four digital files at $120 each) to reach the $1440 value.

Tip Don't use the word savings because it can devalue what clients are receiving. When selling luxury, pointing out added value is a better approach.

As the final piece of each collection, include an incentive to buy additional products. To cap off Collection 1, for example, I offer 10 percent off additional à la carte items. Collection 2 offers an additional 20 percent off, and Collection 2 increases the offer to 50 percent off. These are suggestions; feel free to offer whatever incentive feels best to you! Just be careful that you aren't overly generous (such as discounting more than 50 percent) or stingy (giving only 10 percent to Collection 3).

Remember, these discounts are a bonus for you to get additional sales, so think creatively. Consider selling an additional portrait session to your client by reminding him he can use the discount toward the purchase of his next session fee! Or, you could give your client a certificate allowing him to use the additional discount for an entire year for re-ordering prints. Most clients won't take you up on the offer, but it makes you look good by offering an additional generosity feature. Not to mention that it's a great way to pick up an additional sale or book another session: E-mail your client with a session reminder card two to three months before that one-year certificate expires, saying something like "Just wanted to let you know that your 20 percent discount is about to expire, and I didn't want it to slip away before you had the chance to order more prints or put it toward your next session fee." This a great way to keep marketing to clients without appearing pushy because you are giving them additional courtesy service and taking care of them. Making life easier for the client, that's luxury customer service!

Example collections with specialty items

The examples in the "Collections with Specialty Items" sidebar add canvas prints and albums to the collections and use price points based on 25 percent, 75 percent, and 125 percent increases over the example MOR of $1500. For comparison, the gift print price for this example is $55, digital files sell for $165 apiece, and specialty items are marked up at 5.5 times the gift print price. These collections are designed for a more established business that consistently brings in clients through its marketing efforts and is becoming less sporadic. Notice that Collection 3, the biggest collection, offers basically double the contents of the smallest, Collection 1. This is when upselling is really magical.

COLLECTIONS WITH SPECIALTY ITEMS

$1500 MOR, gift print $55, digital file $165, specialty markup 5.5×

Collection 1, $1875 (à la carte value of $2350)

- 12 gift prints
- Choice of 1 canvas or 3 wall prints (20×30 or smaller)
- Choice of 6 digital files or 1 canvas or 3 wall prints (20×30 or smaller)
- 10 percent off additional à la carte products

Collection 2, $2625 (à la carte value of $4700)

- 12 gift prints
- Choice of 2 canvases or 6 wall prints (20×30 or smaller)
- Choice of 6 digital files or 1 canvas or 3 wall prints (20×30 or smaller)
- 10×10 session album
- 20 percent off additional à la carte products

Collection 3, $3375 (à la carte value of $6060)

- 12 gift prints
- Choice of 3 canvases or 9 wall prints (20×30 or smaller)
- All-inclusive digital files (plus set of 4×6 proofs)
- 10×10 session album
- 50 percent off additional à la carte products

Again, I built the collections with a gift print base, but this time I just put the same number of gift prints in each collection and chose to build by progressively adding specialty items. For example, Collection 1 contains a canvas because that's what ideally I want to sell to all my clients, Collection 2 stacks on a second canvas, and Collection 3 increases the offer to three.

Not everyone is a canvas fan, however, so I offer the equivalent value in wall prints as a choice each time. It's a fantastic way to make your collections flexible without you having to deal with the headache of clients asking for unanticipated swaps and changes. They can basically customize the collections; meanwhile, your cost of goods and collection price remains the same. Offering a choice of equivalent value keeps ordering sessions simple and reduces the frustration for you and your client.

tip If someone wants to buy a larger size than what you have in the collection, make it easy for the client. For instance, if she wants to upgrade the 20×30 canvas for a 24×30 canvas, that's just a $50 difference (see Table 3.3), which is easy for you to add on to the final total.

All three collections in this group also contain digital files, but notice Collection 1 offers the option of receiving an additional canvas or three wall prints in place of the digitals. Additional trade-offs like this are great to put in the collection price list, because clients *love* seeing they have a choice. And they are not overwhelming because there isn't a lot of options you are offering them.

Collection 2 contains everything Collection 1 offered, plus an additional canvas (or three wall prints) and a session album to build the value. For purposes of calculating the equivalent à la carte value, note that the session album assumes a $300 cost of goods and a 5.5 times markup, bringing its à la carte cost to $1650. The incentive for additional sales also increased to 20 percent from Collection 1's 10 percent.

Collection 3 adds a third canvas, as well as the all-inclusive digital files with the set of printed proofs. Collection 3 is basically your dream client session. They buy (and get) everything: gift prints to give away, a wall gallery, all the digital files, and a session album. For the client that wants it all, it's the perfect collection to have. And while your dream client is in a spending mood, you also offer 50 percent off additional à la carte products or a later session fee.

Example digital-focused collections

The sidebar "Digital Collections" offers three more sample collections that use 25 percent, 50 percent, and 75 percent increases over an MOR of $1500. This time, however, the collections emphasize digital files. For comparison, the digital file price is $135 apiece, albums are $2000, and 20×30 canvases sell for $700. If you want to make your main focus digital file and album sales and don't like complicated ordering sessions, this group of collections provides a simple solution. Pet photographers often like this option because their clients generally don't want tons and tons of prints.

note If you are selling albums to every client, make sure you have a workflow that you can maintain to keep up the demand. If you spend 10 hours designing an album but have only 10 hours total to dedicate to a client, the collections won't be sustainable.

Every collection in this group includes an increasing number of digital files, as well as a session album. Collections 2 and 3 also offer a choice of canvases or wall prints.

If you're considering this route, be aware that these collections aren't going to be upselling much. Once you sell your digital files and the client has an album, which essentially contains the entire session, the client loses incentive to buy small prints because he thinks he will simply print

DIGITAL COLLECTIONS

$1500 MOR, digital file $135, album $2000, canvas $700 for 20×30

Collection 1, $2000 (à la carte value $2675)

- 10×10 session album
- 5 digital files
- 10 percent off additional à la carte products

Collection 2, $2500 (à la carte value $3510)

- 10×10 session album
- 6 digital files
- Choice of canvas (20×30 or smaller) or 3 wall prints (20×30 or smaller)
- 20 percent off additional à la carte products

Collection 3, $3000 (à la carte value $4750)

- 10×10 session album
- All-Inclusive digital files (plus set of 4×6 proofs)
- Choice of 2 canvases (20×30 or smaller) or 6 wall prints (20×30 or smaller)
- 50 percent off additional à la carte products

the digital files himself. These collections will have lower gift print sales, and you might get the bulk of your sales in that smallest collection. But the benefit to offering these is that they are a ton easier to sell during the order session when walking a client through the choices. There just aren't many options that require client decisions, so your ordering sessions will be simplistic. If you are completely intimidated with in-person ordering sessions, these could be a great choice for you.

Fill your own collections

So there you go. You now know three unique ways of building your collections. Play around with the ideas, and do what feels best for you. As long as you aren't underselling yourself, you really can't screw up what is in the collections. Calculate your cost of goods and remember your budget: Keep the cost of goods at 15 percent or less of the collection's price. That's what matters most.

Don't be afraid to tweak them as you go. The beauty of locking in the price points first is that you have the comfort of stability. You're still not wavering on what you need your sales to be, you're just refining your offer within a collection. Filling your collections is where you get to be creative.

How to present your pricing

Presenting your pricing in a sales session in some ways is another application of reverse engineering. Your sales goal is to achieve that minimum order requirement, so your MOR is your starting point when you sit down with your clients. From there, you can work backward. Instead of trying to build *up* a sale, ask "What would you like to get with your $*[MOR figure]*?" Introduce clients to your price list, show them they can get for their minimum order, and finally suggest the idea of collections if clients want more bang for their buck or have needs that would be satisfied if they spent just a little bit more. But it's important to always address the minimum order requirement first when you are working with the client.

I mention the MOR figure over and over and over in my client workflow so that clients aren't totally freaking during the ordering session because they were unaware of the minimum. Avoid that uncomfortable, awkward situation for both of you by repeating your minimum order requirement throughout the process. Always aim to make the ordering session as stress free and comfortable as possible. You want clients' lasting impressions of you to be positive and supportive to increase the chances of them becoming return clients.

For the same reason, don't want to start your sales sessions by presenting the collections. If clients are mentally prepared to spend the minimum order requirement, presenting collections first risks the client feeling confused at best and forced into buying more at worst. Instead, as you work with them to determine all the items they want, you can then introduce the collections by saying "Here are some other options that I provide for easier ordering and additional value." Don't lead with your collections, but do sell their value in the form of features and benefits.

Show value through features and benefits

Tip If your clients consistently overlook a product or a service that you offer, you need to assess if you aren't adequately communicating its value and benefits or if it truly is something your clients don't want. Surveys again will help you find the answer.

Your presentation of features and benefits is what makes your products sell or get overlooked. If you don't understand the value of what you are selling, your clients definitely will not understand. *Features* are the factual details about the product or service the client is buying, but *benefits* are what sell the product by answering the "What's in it for me?" questions that every buyer asks. Clients want to know, for example, why they should choose your 8×10, luster prints over your competitor's, which are only half the price. The prints' features appear the same, so why are yours better? Benefits answers their whys.

If you are selling only features, then you are requiring your clients to do all the mental work to figure out why these details matter and why they might want that particular feature. It's not just in their best interest but in *yours* as well to draw the mental connections for them. But to do that, you first have to know what those connections (benefits) are. The following sections highlight three steps that will help you define your features and benefits.

Step 1: Get beyond what you think

If you sell from your point of view only, all you are doing is filling in blanks with assumptions. And let's be honest, you're biased toward your products and services you are selling. It doesn't matter what *you* think about what you are selling. Your potential clients care only if you are selling what they want, and your past clients care only if you satisfied your wants. So don't get stuck in a place communicating only your own bias to your marketplace, but do allow others to help you understand what to communicate. Surveys and collecting data aren't sexy, I know. But you need to listen to the marketplace that you want to attract and not just sell them what you *think* they want and need because it makes you happy to do it.

Step 2: Know your clients

Surveys of past clients will give you fantastic words you can use almost verbatim. Remember the sample survey in Chapter 2, "The Ideal Client and Your Marketplace," asked clients to name the best thing about working with you? That "best thing" generally contains your benefits: How did it improve the life of your client? Did you make everything easy-breezy and focused on convenience? Did you offer professional-quality wall gallery designs that made that Pinterest mom's heart go pitter-patter because it was exactly what she was envisioning and you helped her realize her dream? Did you capture the last moments for a family and their beloved pet before it passed, showing their strong emotional ties? Your past clients can tell you the benefits without your having to guess.

If you don't have past clients, there's another way: Use market surveys to get into the heads of the marketplace by doing research and finding out *why* potential clients want what they want. Once they give you the data, you can use these benefits to see which you believe will best fit what you are trying to sell. Once you start bringing in clients, then you can update your features and benefits based on data from actual clients and improve the way you are communicating what you are selling. The more you rely on what your clients are saying and not just on assumptions of what you hope your products are providing as benefits, the better you'll be able to sell.

Step 3: Think of benefits as results

Communicating benefits is the most effective when you are communicating those benefits as *results*. Yes, it's beneficial to hire a photographer who comes to your home so you don't have to be inconvenienced by going to a studio location. But what's the result that comes from staying home instead of going to a studio? Or vice versa? There are benefits to both, but the results of each are going to help your client further understand the benefits. You ask this by looking at your benefits and answering the question "What's the best outcome that clients can experienced because of this benefit?"

There's a famous story about how Steve Jobs presented the iPod in the early days of MP3 players. While other manufacturers were meticulously explaining the features of their players, Jobs said "1,000 songs in your pocket." *Boom*—he went straight to the benefits we wanted, and iPods sold.

To put it another way, why do people buy quarter-inch drill bits? In *The Marketing Imagination* (The Free Press, 1983), Theodore Levitt quotes Leo McGinneva as explaining "*They don't want quarter-inch bits. They want quarter-inch holes.*" They buy the bit so they can get the results.

That's what you are marketing when you are communicating to your clients the benefits of hiring you and buying from you. Your features are what you sell, your benefit is what your customers do with their experience.

Define your features and benefits

Communicating features and benefits is an art form that can be super challenging but is something that you have to be make a priority to do constantly. Everything that is a part of you and your business has features that you can communicate to clients. Tell them what about you is so special and the benefits they can enjoy as a result. To do so, you must first identify them yourself, so analyze everything: the products you sell, your session fee, your pre-session consultation, your session, your client workflow, your ordering process, your delivery, and your marketing follow-up.

Whenever you are trying to sell something, make sure that you are specific about the features and the benefits of each thing. For example, here's how you can focus on both features and benefits of a canvas:

> "Here is a product that you won't have to feel guilty about spending money on because it sits in a box in your closet and never makes it on the wall. You can immediately bring it home, hang it on the wall without the additional expense and delay of framing. Life gets in the way sometimes, and it's difficult to make it a priority to get the framing done. By the time you make it a priority, you're feeling remorse that so much time has passed, and now it seems outdated and maybe it's just time to get pictures updated. When you get them on the wall immediately, you'll be able to enjoy the money spent and have that comfort that you don't have to feel guilty over another product sitting in a box that never got framed. And with a canvas, it's nice and light so that it's easy to hang without any help or special tools, or even those little picture hooks you never can find when you need them. It'll save you the hassle of remembering to buy more and the frustration of finding a pile of hanger packages, after you already opened the new one."

Yes, it sounds slightly like a sales pitch, but you have to get over that because you *are* selling. At the same time, you're touching on the emotional elements, such as reducing guilt, regret, and remorse; providing simplicity; saving money and time; plus increasing satisfaction, comfort, and enjoyment of products. These claims might sound a little outrageous, but they are all completely true. When you piece everything together, sometimes you don't realize the effect that benefits can have.

It takes a lot of practice getting used to talking this way and communicating it, so don't get overwhelmed or discouraged when it seems incredibly awkward to do at first. The Features and Benefits Worksheet will help you get your thoughts in order, and then you can explain features and benefits on your website, in blog posts, during your sales session, and more. There are so many opportunities!

Entice clients with website copy

Website copy is one of the most neglected elements for sales conversions that turn interest into bookings. Generally, the lack of copy is based on a lot of false assumptions and beliefs. Here are the most common mistakes:

- Omitting pricing on the website
- Listing a session fee with no explanation of what a session fee covers, completely lacking all the features and benefits.
- Relying on imagery alone to sell instead of copy with heavy image-based websites
- Not communicating the value in hiring you instead of another photographer

The sections that follow will help you avoid these pitfalls and improve your website copy's effectiveness.

Repeatedly communicate your pricing

When someone visits your website, one of the first places he will go is your pricing information. If it's missing or inadequate, potential clients won't contact you. If there is any doubt in his mind over whether he can afford you, he's not going to take the time to contact you, which means a lost sale if you fit his budget perfectly!

Don't miss that sale: Devote an entire page to your pricing so potential and current clients can see every single detail about the costs of your collections and prints. Not only does this save you time responding to tire kickers, a page dedicated to your full pricing also is a great way to reduce information overload when you introduce your pricing to the new client. For example, your session page could list your session fee and basic pricing information and include a link that says, "For more detailed information on pricing, click here." This way, you can satisfy the person who just wants the basics without overwhelming him with prices for albums, canvases, and collections before he has an emotional connection to the images. At the same time, the person who wants to know every single detail can have it all with a simple click.

note For additional advice on pricing and websites, see the section "Pricing on your website attracts ideal clients" in Chapter 2.

FEATURES AND BENEFITS WORKSHEET

What makes me unique, from start to finish?

Sessions

Feature	Benefit/Emotional Value/Result

Services

Feature	Benefit/Emotional Value/Result

Products

Feature	Benefit/Emotional Value/Result

Ordering Process

Feature	Benefit/Emotional Value/Result

Client Workflow

Feature	Benefit/Emotional Value/Result

Locations

Feature	Benefit/Emotional Value/Result

Other

Feature	Benefit/Emotional Value/Result

If you are constantly changing your pricing, stop. It's unprofessional to change your pricing constantly, so don't make that a habit. Your collection price points, and à la carte pricing needs to stay solid. Create your pricing, stick with it, and if something is failing after a season of testing, *then* change it. As soon as you do change it, post it on your site. Likewise, when you tweak what's *in* your collections, update your website to reflect their new contents, as well as their equivalent à la carte value.

Explain your benefits

The person landing on your website wants a photographer; she doesn't need to be educated on the benefits of having custom photography as soon as she gets there. From its first page, your site needs to use words that immediately communicate to your clients what you do that makes you the best choice and why—your features and benefits.

Your website copy doesn't have to be elaborate and fancy; it just needs to be direct and point to what makes you awesome. What convinces these website shoppers that *you* are the one for them always takes place in the copy? It doesn't happen in your portfolio and galleries. Your focus needs to be on selling the features and benefits of what *you* uniquely do and what makes you stand out.

To hone your website copy skills, do some market research on how websites in other industries sell products and services. Avoid discount-driven sites and look for sites that handle non-necessities or emotional-need products. (See the sidebar "Juicy Examples" for one such industry.) Make mental notes of what you see that makes you want to buy immediately or at least sign up for a mailing list or request a free introductory product offering. What website elements communicated an urgency to you or created a hunger for more? Was the information focused more on features (what you were getting) or benefits (how the product or service would transform your life)? Was it detailed or vague? As you gain a sense of what resonates (and what doesn't), you'll be able to better communicate with your clients via your own website.

JUICY EXAMPLES

Here's a quick example market for you to analyze: juicing. Juice cleansing is a huge craze, and it has amazing benefits. Some people aren't good potential clients, however, because it is outside of their price point of affordability. They won't see benefits to their lives because they don't feel that they are lacking enough in that area to have a strong need for it. After the juice bar craze started, companies looked for how they could better diversify and set themselves apart from the crowd. Take a look at how some use their website copy to convey key features and benefits succinctly:

- **BluePrint Cleanse (http://blueprintcleanse.com). The Original. The Best.** The company owns its niche and grabs the top by saying "We were here first." The sales feature is that BluePrint Cleanse is the original juice company, while the stated benefit is that it's the best. The short phrases imply that's all you need to know.
- **Cooler Cleanse (http://coolercleanse.com). Detox to your door.** The company says it's the best for delivery. The obvious detox in a bottle (feature), which has the benefit of being delivered to your door, meaning it's super easy for you, no excuses. Cooler Cleanse also offers high-quality organic juice (feature), which nourishes humans, plus protects and preserves the planet. (Those are mighty bold benefit claims, right?)
- **Arden's Garden (http://www.ardensgarden.com). We're more than just juice.** Not only does the company say that it offers more than just juice, it also ships its juice and smoothies frozen instead of fresh, which doesn't put you on a time crunch to start your cleanse the minute it arrives on your doorstep (feature). This better longevity means customers have less worry about expiration and waste (benefit).

For someone who isn't familiar with juicing, not knowing where to begin or which company (let alone which product) to choose can be overwhelming. To convert a looker into a buyer and possibly even a loyal, repeat client, companies must clearly communicate their unique features and benefits in a compelling way.

Describe a session

Make sure that your website copy includes what clients can expect in a typical session. Describe the experience from start to finish. You could even include a video on your website as an engaging way to explain your beautifully choreographed client workflow or to show curious clients what goes on behind the scenes. The possibilities are endless for showing the features and benefits of working with you.

Do be sure to list or link to your pricing information, such as the session fee, the minimum order requirement, the starting point for collections, but don't lead with your prices. You don't want to risk raising doubts or negative feelings about affordability before people fully understand what they will be getting. Build a hunger for the service, features, and benefits you offer, then explain the costs involved.

Picture your pricing information

So, I've convinced you that displaying your pricing on your website is beneficial, but you're still wondering how to display it? Here's a sample hierarchical layout for your session information and details page; think of it as a skeleton you can flesh out:

- Session information

  Features and benefits

  Details of a typical session
- Session fee $*[price]*

  Features and benefits
- Minimum order requirement $*[price]*
- Staring price for prints $*[price]*

  Link to the full price list

  Or, link to a page that requires visitors to provide an e-mail address to receive the full price list (this option also builds your e-mail list for marketing)
- Contact information (to schedule a session right away)

In-person vs. online sales

When I started out in business, I relied on my website to handle all of my portrait sales. I averaged between three and five sessions per week during the busy season and steadily did at least two per week when it was slow. Because of everything else going on in my life, I couldn't imaging handling in-person sales without over-extending myself. I did well with online sales because I spent a lot of time working with my clients to walk them through the process and assist them. When I got my studio space, I started bringing in larger sales per client and reducing the number of sales sessions I was doing. I could have handled the time demand of doing in-person sales at that point, but my online sales were working so well that I just stuck with them.

It ended up being a big mistake. My sales were stuck in a rut. Colleagues, I found, were making double to triple the sales average in person as I was making online. Given the amount of time I was already devoting to assisting clients online, a few simple tweaks in my lifestyle could have gained me the additional time I needed to feel comfortable with in-person sales.

Weigh the costs

My arbitrary decision to do what worked best for me and not what was best for my client ended up losing me potential money, as well as stronger loyalty with my clients. The element of working with a person face to face is not about a calculator whittling away at a wish list like it is online. In person, you are able to dig deep into what the client wants and needs. The more you learn about your clients, the more effective you can be at reaching out to potential clients because you better understand their reasons for hiring you and purchasing your work. You aren't going to learn anything about your clients from your side of a computer screen. It takes rubbing shoulders and watching them make decisions right in front of you.

tip Imperfect pricing for in-person sales yields better results than perfect pricing for online sales.

To understand what you could possibly be losing per month, consider an example. Your goal is eight clients a month and you average $500 per online sale. In-person sales could bring in an extra $250 per client, meaning an extra $2000 per month. Or, suppose your $1000 online sales could bring in an additional $500 as in-person sales; that's $4000 more per month for the same eight clients. The money really adds up. Even if you have to pay a little more per month for child-care or other part-time help, the extra income is enough to be a worthwhile trade-off.

The worst part about sticking with online sales was that I missed an important opportunity to make happier clients by selling them *exactly* what they wanted instead of what they thought they needed while purchasing their goods online. Think about it, which would *you* rather do: work with a professional who can show you examples and provide a plan for how to best use the products all while all working within your budget in less than two hours or figure it out for yourself online, putting things in your cart and taking them out for a week while you mull over your options?

Ask your clients, but ask them in a marketing-savvy manner. Don't include a question on your survey like "Do you want a sales session in person or online?" Clients will answer "online," because no one likes the feeling of being sold to. But, you could ask "Do you value having guidance through the ordering process, or are you a do-it-yourself type?" Most people appreciate the help. Find out which your clients prefer, so you know exactly what they want.

Sell the benefits

In-person sales can become a benefit to the client, just like all the other features and benefits of your business. You sell the sales session to your client by communicating the worth in working further with you. If she has a jam-packed schedule, for instance, you can benefit her by reducing the time the process takes and avoid the stress of rushing to meet an online gallery expiration deadline. Remember your research! Strive to better understand the needs and struggles of your clients and then draw up a list of benefits of how an ordering session can help solve some of these problems.

Every time you provide this luxury customer service, word-of-mouth marketing will build. When you spend one-on-one presentation time with a client, you provide more of a service than just photography. You are giving them peace of mind. You give them convenience. You help them not to waste their money with images that wind up in shoeboxes.

Do not solely rely on word-of-mouth, however. Many photographers make the mistake of assuming that their clients and potential clients know all the benefits of in-person sales and so neglect to mention this service in their website copy. Every time you miss the opportunity to share features and benefits with your clients about what it is like to work with you, you further add confusion of exactly what it is that they are paying you for.

If you sell in person, showcase all that it involves from start to finish, outline the problems that it solves and the multiple benefits, and then market those things through your website as a part of the process of hiring you. Give your audience another reason to choose you and make sure that your website copy tells them all about that one-on-one awesomeness. Doing so will help them perceive further value to that session fee that they are paying you, as well as help them trust that you will reduce the stress and anxiety about the ordering process.

5

PRICING CONSISTENCY FOR WEDDINGS AND OTHER SPECIALTY SESSIONS

Some specialty sessions won't fit neatly into the portrait pricing model discussed so far. For instance, weddings aren't like the typical portrait session. The locations are determined by the client, the products are different, the amount of shooting time and post work is completely different, there can be more than you working the event, you don't get the opportunity to reshoot or extend the shooting time, and so on. You are on their clock; ultimately, they call the shots, and you are paid to show up and document. Likewise, mini-sessions, a holiday season favorite for many clients, are not simply scaled-down portrait sessions but require their own approach to keep what can be an excellent marketing opportunity from becoming a drain on your time and resources.

Although the pricing model may be different, the strategy for pricing weddings and mini-sessions should be familiar: Know your clients' wants and needs and know your marketplace. Marketplace research is vital because wedding pricing can vary greatly without a consistent trend in the industry. By listening to your own research, you can ensure your wedding and mini-session prices *complement* and are *consistent* with your portrait-pricing model.

Build from your current prices

Before you take on that wedding or those mini-sessions, it is of the utmost importance to have your portrait pricing firmly in place as an established foundation to build from. Clients won't balk at the prices that you set for weddings or mini-sessions if they tie into the portrait prices already on your website and all the prices send a consistent message about your business. Consistency builds trust (more on this later), while wildly varying prices, or those with no logical basis, breed suspicion. If you asked a local, midpriced restaurant about its catering, for example, and were quoted fast-food cheap or blasphemously expensive prices, you would question why those prices were so far out of line. When it comes to a client's perspective, that question alone can make the person think twice about your services. This is not a good thing.

Having your pricing established helps you in two ways. By being up front and honest about what your services are worth, you assure potential clients that you're not hiding anything or planning to pop some hidden charges in when they're not paying attention. It also gives you a general framework that helps you establish prices when the opportunity for specialty sessions arises. Consistency gives you, and your clients, peace of mind about what you will be offering and what level of services to expect. The more comfortable your clients are with "who you are" in your pricing, the more confident they will be to choose you.

Three common wedding models

When pricing weddings, the model you choose should be one that provides the best result for both you and your client, just like with portrait sessions. But the difference here is that the creative choices are substantially easier, simply because there isn't a lot of flexibility in what you can offer in your wedding packages.

Most people hiring a wedding photographer know exactly what they want, which is practically a standard: formal and informal bridal party portraits, ceremony coverage, reception coverage, and perhaps photobooth shots, which are becoming increasingly popular. You can't get too creative in what you offer to your clients because the session is based on an event at which all of the elements are outside of your control. You don't really get to pick the locations, the outfits, or the style, unlike a typical portrait session for which you can coach the client in what to wear, the best locations to choose, the look and feel of the session, and more.

There are three common approaches to wedding photography: shoot and burn, studio, and digital delivery. Let's take a closer look at each model:

- **Shoot-and-burn photographers** are all about their rock-bottom prices, delivering their images on a USB thumb drive or a CD. They have gotten a bad rap in the industry simply because they are the least professional in customer service and quality of work, as well as have the least amount of client interaction from start to finish. Not all shoot-and-burn photographers are haunting Craigslist.com seeking to take advantage of budget-tight brides, but the truth of the matter is that you get what you pay for. Not everyone can afford to spend more than $1000 on wedding photography and not everyone values or is capable of affording the best of the best, so these photographers will always be around. The shoot-and-burn photographer is not devaluing the industry any more than the reputation or sales of authentic Louis Vuitton handbags are hurt by knock-offs. If your goal is to be a luxury studio as we discussed previously, however, then you already know this is not your model.
- **Studio photographers** may or may not have actual studio space. I refer to them as studio photographers simply because they set themselves up to serve a more local marketplace with more of a come-to-me business model. Studio photographers generally offer in-person pre-wedding consultations and in-person ordering sessions. Because studio photographers have more client interaction, taking the time to get to know their clients' needs, they develop stronger client relationships. The time that is being spent working with clients one on one before and after the wedding builds to a stronger level of trust, which improves your chances of getting word-of-mouth marketing. Plus, this model offers tangible products, such as albums and canvases, which are considered far more valuable today than digital products. Conversely, studio photographers are limited in profitability in the sense that their time involvement is higher, both in client interaction and in product creation. Their cost of goods will be higher as well, because of the costs of renting or owning a studio space.
- **Digital-delivery photographers** deliver images digitally through downloads and offer no tangible products. Although the digital-delivery model relies on website, e-mail, and phone communication rather than face-to-face interaction with the clients, you can design a relation-building client workflow focused on customer service that still feels luxurious and high end. At the same time, the digital-delivery model cuts back overhead expenses substantially because you no longer need to pay for a studio space, product materials, or shipping. In some states, delivering totally digitally also means you do not have to pay state taxes on the total sale, which can mean a savings of hundreds

tip Consult www.taxjar.com/states to check your state's laws on taxing digitally delivered products to help determine whether having a digital model would be beneficial for your business.

to thousands of dollars per year. You'll also lower your workload by eliminating the need for album design and such. Unfortunately, you also limit the "wow factor" you can offer and your opportunities for upselling. Digital-delivery photographers are hired on a flat rate, which may mean a lower total sale. Unlike studio photographers, they won't benefit from impulse spending at the order session when the client sees the images presented are better than expected.

In my opinion, the studio and digital-delivery models are equal in their opportunity for profitability, and I have seen both work phenomenally well. The studio model provides a personal touch throughout the process, which can be reassuring amid the wedding chaos. Meanwhile, digital-delivery photographers are often more appealing to destination wedding clients or those who aren't local to you for convenient in-person consultations, ordering, or delivery. As always, research your marketplace and analyze your needs and your clients' needs to determine your best course.

How to price your weddings

The first step, as when addressing any pricing, is to determine what your clients really want. Do your wedding clients *really* want a 30×40 canvas? Do they even want a canvas at all? Do they want 4×6 proofs of every image, or would they be happier just to have the digital files? Tweak the surveys in Chapter 2, "The Ideal Client and Your Marketplace," to research what your wedding clients really, truly want for you to sell to them and what they value most. Collect the data. Don't just look around to see what other photographers are offering in their packages. You don't know for a fact that their packages are working or if their clients are thrilled with everything they are getting (or not getting) in those packages. With weddings, you could be giving away too much in cost of goods by providing printed proofs and wall galleries when your clients would be just as happy with digital files and an album. Research is too important a step to skip.

Consistent and simple

Pricing weddings can be tricky, tricky work. If you compare prices among your competitors, you'll see there just isn't a perfect, one-size-fits-all model. Not to mention, the services you offer for your weddings can range drastically based on travel fees, photobooths, the need to hire second shooters, and more.

If you are doing weddings as a side offering rather than your main business, you'll want to be sure your wedding pricing is consistent with the rest of your portrait offerings. The best way is to use the same method used to create your standard portrait pricing: Keep your cost of goods sold (COGS) under the 15 percent of each wedding package's sale price and offer no more than three packages. This way you will be able to ensure that your weddings are always profitable and you don't need nickel and dime every single little detail. Also, as with portrait collections, your wedding packages should be "stackable" with the more expensive packages building on and expanding the contents of the base package.

note See Chapter 3, "Reverse Engineering Your Pricing," for more detail on using COGS and pricing for albums.

Count your hours

The "Basic Wedding Pricing for Studio Photographers" and "Basic Wedding Pricing for Digital Delivery" worksheets use your hourly value to build prices for three levels of wedding packages. To do this effectively, you have to know exactly how much time you spend on your clients at every stage—both shooting the wedding and behind the scenes. It's always best to over-estimate than under-estimate the amount of time that you expect to spend; if you guess that you will spend only 10 hours of editing and it ends up taking more than 30, you're going to lose money.

note The examples in this chapter are focused on the most simplistic pricing scenarios that don't include a second shooter, travel fees, and so on. Nor are the worksheets broken down to the minute detail that may be necessary if your weddings are the highest percentage of your client sales.

Once you have a few weddings under your belt, you will gain a better idea of how much time the process will take. If you haven't shot a wedding before, be prepared to probably be off in your estimation with your first few weddings and then plan to tweak as you go. I highly recommend tracking the time that you spend to get the most realistic count of all that goes into the process that you are selling.

After you create your collections, always double-check that your COGS falls under the 15 percent of your prices. Usually you will find that the hourly value will cover the costs and keep you under the 15 percent. If you exceed that limit, however, you may need to consider either choosing a lower-priced album or increasing your prices.

note To complete the "Basic Wedding Pricing" worksheets, you will need your Hourly Value, which is line F in the "Your Numbers Bible" worksheet in Chapter 1, "Getting Started."

As you gain experience and want to expand your wedding services, be sure to factor in additional expenses, such as travel or photobooth costs, as you go based on demand. For now, the worksheets are a place to start so you always have something immediately ready whenever you get an inquiry for a wedding. You can be confident that the job will be well worth your time because you know exactly what your time is worth.

BASIC WEDDING PRICING FOR STUDIO PHOTOGRAPHERS

Package 1

Contents: _____ Hours of Shooting, Digital Files, Proof Set

Package 1 estimated hours per client:

____

Customer service and communication

____

Shooting

____

Editing

____

Sales

____

Packaging

____

Delivering

____

Total estimated hours per client (TEH)

____

Price:

______ (TEH) × ______ (Hourly Value) =
______ (Price of Package 1)

Package 2

Contents: ________ Hours of Shooting, Digital Files, Proof Set, Session Album

Package 2 estimated hours per client:

____

Customer service and communication

____

Shooting

____

Editing

____

Sales

____

Packaging

____

Delivering

____

Total estimated hours per client (TEH)

____

Price:

______ (TEH) × ______ (Hourly Value) =
______ (Price of Package 2)

Package 3

Contents: Choice of Specialty Session, ______ Hours of Shooting, Specialty Session Album, Wedding Album Digital Files, Proof Set

Package 3 estimated hours per client:

____
Customer service and communication

____
Shooting

____
Editing

____
Sales

____
Packaging

____
Delivering

____
Total estimated hours per client (TEH)

____

Price:

______ (TEH) × ______ (Hourly Value) = ______ (Price of Package 3)

À la carte Additional Specialty Sessions:

Engagement session price:

______ (Total Hours) × ______ (Hourly Value) = ______ (Price)

Bridal session price:

______ (Total Hours) × ______ (Hourly Value) = ______ (Price)

Day-after session price:

______ (Total Hours) × ______ (Hourly Value) = ______ (Price)

Rehearsal dinner coverage price:

______ (Total Hours) × ______ (Hourly Value) = ______ (Price)

Photobooth price:

______ (Total Hours) × ______ (Hourly Value) = ______ (Price)

BASIC WEDDING PRICING FOR DIGITAL-DELIVERY PHOTOGRAPHERS

Package 1

Contents: _____ Hours of Shooting, Digital Files for Download

Package 1 estimated hours per client:

____

Customer service and communication

____

Shooting

____

Editing

____

Total estimated hours per client (TEH)

____

Price:

______ (TEH) × ______ (Hourly Value) = ______ (Price of Package 1)

Package 2

Contents: ________ Hours of Shooting, Digital Files for Download

Package 2 estimated hours per client:

____

Customer service and communication

____

Shooting

____

Editing

____

Total estimated hours per client (TEH)

____

Price:

______ (TEH) × ______ (Hourly Value) = ______ (Price of Package 2)

tip For tips on contracts for wedding sessions and more, see Chapter 6, "Troubleshooting Guide."

Package 3

Contents: Choice of Specialty Session, ______ Hours of Shooting, Specialty Session Album, Wedding Album Digital Files, Proof Set

Package 3 estimated hours per client:

____

Customer service and communication

____

Shooting

____

Editing

____

Total estimated hours per client (TEH)

____

Price:

______ (TEH) × ______ (Hourly Value) = ______ (Price of Package 3)

À la carte Additional Specialty Sessions:

Engagement session price:

______ (Total Hours) × ______ (Hourly Value) = ______ (Price)

Bridal session price:

______ (Total Hours) × ______ (Hourly Value) = ______ (Price)

Day-after session price:

______ (Total Hours) × ______ (Hourly Value) = ______ (Price)

Rehearsal dinner coverage price:

______ (Total Hours) × ______ (Hourly Value) = ______ (Price)

Photobooth price:

______ (Total Hours) × ______ (Hourly Value) = ______ (Price)

EXAMPLE WEDDING PRICE SHEET

So, what does a studio photographer's worksheet look like translated to packages and prices? I'll show you. For this example layout, assume your hourly value is $150 per hour and the total estimated time takes into account both shooting the images and your processing workflow. (The cost of goods and products will all come in under your 15 percent COGS, so you don't need to factor products into the service.)

Package 1: $2100
(4 hours of shooting plus 10 hours of client workflow; 14 total hours)

- 4 hours of continuous wedding day coverage
- All-inclusive digital files
- Proof set (4×6 prints)
- 10 percent off additional à la carte items

Package 2: $3000
(6 hours of shooting plus 14 hours of client workflow; 20 total hours)

- 6 hours of continuous wedding day coverage
- All-inclusive digital files
- Proof set (4×6 prints)
- Session album
- 20% off additional à la carte items

Package 3: $3900
(8 hours of shooting plus 18 hours of client workflow; 26 total hours)

- Specialty session: choice of engagement session, bridal session, rehearsal dinner coverage, day-after session, or photobooth
- 8 hours of continuous wedding day coverage
- All-inclusive digital files
- Proof set (4×6 prints)
- Wedding album
- Engagement album
- 50% off additional à la carte items

For additional à la carte items, use the price sheet for wall prints and canvases that you created in Chapter 3.

How to price your mini-sessions

Mini-sessions are a sample of, not a substitute for, your signature experience. At their best, they are a special offering that allows new clients to experience your services at a cheaper rate—an enticement to hire you again at the full rate after an enjoyable session with impressive results.

The operative part is "mini." Don't kill your full-priced sessions by doing too much for your mini-sessions. If a client can get 30 images out of a 20-minute session, why hire you to do a "full" session? Even if a session results in 30 strong images, present only a few. Showing more does not guarantee a larger sale; it basically guarantees only that you edit more, overwhelm your clients, and sabotage your mini-as-marketing efforts. Mini-sessions are best kept short all around: 15 minutes for the session and six to eight images for the presentation.

tip Space those 15-minute mini-sessions 30 minutes apart in case a client is late or you have a session with a difficult subject.

Your pricing should be the same. Don't discount it for your mini-sessions, but do offer smaller packages and collections. Reduce your minimum order requirement by about 70 percent for mini-sessions. Shrink a $500 MOR to $150 (500 – [500 × 0.7] or 500 × 0.3), for example, and a $250 MOR to $75. Likewise, your fee for a mini-session should be 25 percent of your full-session fee, but no less than $50.

tip Shortcut for the math-phobic: If your session fee $200 or less, then your mini-session fee will be the $50 minimum.

Keep your collection contents super simple, as well: small prints (8×10s and smaller) and digital files only. Remember to limit the options to get the biggest sale. The "Mini-Session Pricing" worksheet will help you get started.

Marketing for mini-sessions

To be successful with mini-sessions, you need a bit more preparation than simply calculating your prices. You need a plan, especially if you want to be ready for the clients who want "just a few photos" for the holidays.

Begin early— September or early October at the latest—and find a partner in crime. As you look for local businesses to collaborate with, think beyond your niche a little. Perhaps that super cool pet store would like to partner to promote pet and parent sessions. Children's boutiques are an obvious target for kids and family sessions, but remember, singles like to get dressed for holiday photos too. What about joining forces with a hair salon or spa? Coffee shops (envision steaming mugs of hot chocolate and a family snuggled around a booth), floral shops (the staff will be used to designing gorgeous holiday scenes), and even lingerie shops have potential. Get creative, and get connected with a local business.

MINI-SESSION PRICING

Price all à la carte prints and digital files the same as for your full sessions

Session Fee (25% of your full-session fee; minimum $50): ____________________

Minimum Order Requirement (30% of full-session MOR): ____________________

Collection Increases: 25%, 50%, 75% above mini-session MOR

Collection 1: ________ (mini MOR) × 1.25 = ________ (Collection 1 Price)

Collection 2: ________ (mini MOR) × 1.5 = ________ (Collection 2 Price)

Collection 3: ________ (mini MOR) × 1.75 = ________ (Collection 3 Price)

EXAMPLE MINI-SESSION PRICE SHEET

If your full-price MOR was $1000, what would your mini-session collections look like? To begin, your Mini MOR would be $300. Also assume that your gift prints would cost $40, meaning digital files would $120 apiece, a 16×20 would be $120, and all-inclusive digital files (per file price × 3) total slightly higher than the MOR at $360. The collections would look like this:

Collection 1: $375 (à la carte value $480)

- 6 gift prints
- 2 digital files
- 10% off additional à la carte prints

Collection 2: $450 (à la carte value $660)

- 8 gift prints
- 1 wall print (16×20 or smaller)
- 2 digital files
- 20% off additional à la carte prints

Collection 3: $525 (à la carte value $960)

- 10 gift prints
- 2 wall prints (16×20 or smaller)
- All-inclusive digital files
- Proof set (4×6 prints)

50% off additional à la carte prints

Entice and sign a partner

So, you've found the perfect business—lucrative connection, killer natural light, excellent shooting location—now how do you approach the owners to make them want to collaborate with you? You make it beneficial for *them.*

Talk to the owner in person. Call him, set up a time to chat over coffee or lunch, and show him your suggestions. Have a vision, and pitch the vision to the business owner in front of you. Offer him half of each session fee that comes in, or even the entire fee if you really want to entice him. For every single one of his clients that he convinces to book a session, you have to give him something to make opening his business to you worthwhile. The owner and his staff are going to market you to their clients, so you should not expect them to do this for free.

Giving the owner a portion of each session fee means you'll need to unbundle your holiday session offerings if you currently offer an all-inclusive price to your clients. Instead, charge a small session fee ($50 or 25 percent of your regular session fee, whichever is *more*) and then create holiday packages on the back end, once your clients have seen their images. There's no way for that poor mom to know whether she wants Collection 1, 2, or 3 without seeing the images. A scowling, bratty child means she'll go for the lowest-cost option. If her daughter was a cooperative angel, on the other hand, she'll spring for the most comprehensive collection.

Once you agree to working with a business, draw up a contract and both of you sign the agreement. Write down the agreed-upon dates, the percentage of the session fee you'll give the business for allowing you to shoot in there, and when you'll deliver that payment. Be very specific. The professionalism you display will build the business owner's confidence in you. Do not ever give him a reason to regret agreeing to collaborate with you. Just as a business can help build your client base, a disgruntled owner can also destroy your marketing efforts and make your name mud.

Get promoting and share the love

Be as helpful as humanly possible to the other business owner. Put together postcards for the owner to hand out in her store to each customer. You can do some in-store test photos to use as promo images (bonus points if you feature the owner in the shoot). The owner will be much more likely to promote you to her clients when she's gracing the cards. Put both your business names on the card to give it more credibility and further entice the business owner to promote you: "Urban Coffee & Smoky Mountain Photography are offering holiday mini-sessions." Smaller business cards are a great alternative for those who want to tuck information into their back pockets. Be sure to ask whether there's anything else you could provide to help her to promote you. For example, you could supply posters for the front window or a large, mounted sample print to display in the store to help clients envision what you'll be creating.

When you send out promotional materials to your photography clients, promote your partner business as well. Offer bonus coupons or gift certificates for each paid mini-session fee to entice clients into the store. Provide the certificates at your own expense, please; don't ask the owner to give you freebies!

tip Remember, you want at least six weeks of marketing before the sessions to get any new clients to bite. I recommend eight weeks. Giving yourself an insanely small window to promote mini-sessions is only ensuring failure or low turnout.

One year, for example, I gave each person who booked a mini-session a $25 gift certificate to the children's boutique I partnered with. The idea was that the client could put the $25 toward a holiday outfit for the child's session. Those certificates were at my expense, so the boutique owner knew I was serious about promoting her business. Building clients and sales for the business you're working with earns you love from the owner! I reinvested my portion of the session fee back into the store, which blew the owner's mind. I didn't have much money in my business budget at the time, so I only purchased a certificate after a session fee came in. I didn't profit at all from the session fees, as they just covered all the marketing expenses. My profiting goal was for the orders. Yes, it was a risk. But those mini-sessions fed my family through the winter because they were a *huge* success.

Manage client expectations

Managing your clients' expectations is as important to mini-session success as the rest of your marketing efforts. Only happy, satisfied clients return. Create a PDF that outlines what clients can expect, including session time, the number of images you will present, helpful tips to ensure a smooth session, and so on. In addition, include a model release and contract for the client to sign and return to you. Send the PDF to clients who book a session, and make sure you have a printed copy on hand at the time of the session, just in case clients forget to return their contracts.

Manage the client's post-session expectations as well by explaining the online ordering process. Give clients a link to where they can print their holiday cards (spare yourself the agony of doing this on a large scale), and provide a timeline that explains when clients can view proofs on your website, how long clients have to order, and when they can expect to pick up their orders or have them delivered. To facilitate order pickup, arrange a day with the owner of your partner business when you can be on-site for clients to pick up their orders. Schedule pick-up times with all your mini-session clients to avoid walk-in chaos. I've found this to be the easiest method of delivering orders, and it allows you one last bit of face time with each new client!

Build trust with consistency

Whether focusing on weddings, mini-sessions, portraits, or a mix, we all want our potential clients to become current clients and our current clients to become repeat clients. Our clients, meanwhile, want to have the sense that every time they come to us, they will receive the same excellent level of service and stunning images. We really want the same things: trust and consistency.

Everyone knows that building trust with clients is essential if you want to have a successful business. Instinctively, we know that if we lose the trust of our clients, not only do we lose a sale, we also lose word-of-mouth marketing and repeat clients. What isn't so obvious is that maintaining a high standard of consistency in your customer service, products, and pricing will help build that trust with clients.

The benefits of pricing consistency is twofold. Not only does it secure that you are making the same amount of money for the effort in everything that you provide, it most importantly builds trust with your clients by providing consistency in all your services that you offer.

If clients hire you for a mini-session, your full portrait session pricing won't give them sticker shock when they compare the value of what they receive. The same is true for clients hiring you to shoot a wedding. They know they are getting more (or getting less) and that pricing is consistent with what you provide.

Your pricing will either build trust or lose trust with how your client sees you. But that trust has to come from first being created with presenting value. Pricing alone is not enough to create trust; it can only expand it or it can lose it. You must present value to earn that trust in the first place.

THE LOGISTICS OF BOOKING AND ORDERING

Have you given up on or been avoiding holiday-season mini-sessions because dealing with so many clients in such a compressed time is too daunting? Following these simple steps will eliminate the headaches:

1. Create a ledger of all time slots.
2. Take session fees over the phone via PayPal Virtual Terminal or your own credit card terminal. (Yes, e-mailing back and forth may seem easier, but it lacks the personal touch. Use the phone.)
3. Fill in the ledger when a new client has paid the session fee. Write down the contact names, phone numbers, and e-mail addresses, as well as the names of the sessions' subjects.
4. Call the day before the session and remind each client of the time. Make sure you have extra contracts and model releases on hand because people will most likely forget to bring theirs. Have each decision maker sign before you get started.
5. Post *all* mini-session galleries to your website at the same time and plan to remove them all on the same expiration date. This alone will save you lots of hassle.
6. On gallery posting day, call or e-mail each person to explain the session gallery is available for viewing on your website. Remind clients of their ordering timeframe, and let them know they can contact you with any questions that arise.
7. Call or e-mail each person that hasn't yet ordered on the day before galleries expire to remind clients that it's the last day.
8. Send out a notecard to each person who has placed an order, thanking clients and letting them know about how long it will be before they can expect the "Your order is here!" phone call.
9. Include a little something extra in the orders of those who buy your highest mini-session package—a note, a small gift card to the store you were working in, some cookies, some cakes. Make your biggest spenders feel valued; you want them to return!

Above all, give your clients opportunity after opportunity to fall in love with you and to become a lifetime client.

6

TROUBLESHOOTING GUIDE

As you've probably noticed by now, profitability doesn't happen instantly and relies on more than simply good pricing. The first half of this chapter offers some help and advice on all (or at least many) of those other factors: client relations, confidence, marketing, momentum, and more. Plus, in the second half, you'll find recommendations for books, blog posts, e-courses, and vendor websites where you can find even more inspiration and information to help you overcome trouble spots on the road to profitability.

Commonly asked questions

note If you have a question that isn't covered here, please e-mail me at getcaredfor@profitfirstphotography, and I'll be more than happy to help!

Although it may feel like you're the only one struggling with problems while establishing your pricing, chances are another photographer has wrestled with the same thing—chances are I may have, too. The sections that follow answer many of the most commonly asked questions that pricing leads to: how to make the transition to your new pricing, what to do when people aren't willing to pay your prices, how to deal with deadline-challenged clients, whether to offer online or in-person ordering (and how to make the most of each). I'll even help you with what to say to relatives who want to take advantage of your services.

How do I make the transition to my new pricing?

You can transition into your new pricing in two ways: You can rip off your old pricing like a Band-Aid and replace it with your new pricing—whoosh, just like that—or you can transition gradually.

The advantage of the "Band-Aid" method is that your transition will be faster, and each of your new clients will be immediately bringing in what your business needs to sustain. It's scary to make a huge leap, however, and if you aren't confident in the leap, your clients are going to sense that. If you don't believe in your pricing, convincing your audience that you are worth every penny is going to be even harder.

For a more gradual transition, you can ease into your new pricing by offering it at a discount for a limited time. This will acclimate your clients to the direction that your business is headed by showing them what your full pricing will be and building awareness that you are going to be full-price eventually. Be aware, however, that early discounts may attract lower-paying clients who won't stay with you after you go to full pricing.

If you opt to transition gradually, give yourself no more than five months to do so. Anything longer than that won't make sense to your audience because it will look more like a bait and switch or hesitation. You want to present your transition confidently; map out a solid schedule of dates, such as the following:

- **March**: Receive 50 percent off purchase
- **April**: Receive 40 percent off purchase
- **May**: Receive 30 percent off purchase
- **June**: Receive 20 percent off purchase
- **July**: Receive 10 percent off purchase

Keep your session fee at full price, and discount your MOR by the schedule. If your new, full-price MOR is typically $1000, for March it would be only $500, for instance. (You can offer a discounted session fee as well, but realize that all that profit will come out of your pocket!)

Whatever schedule you choose, set solid dates and *stick to them*. Whenever you discount what you are offering, you want to make sure that you are not attracting deal-seekers only, or else you will find yourself working with people who might try pushing boundaries to get even more out of you.

How do I tell my past clients about my new pricing?

Every time we come up with a new pricing structure, we face the question of how to launch it and to notify past clients about price increases. Outside the photographic industry, however, it's pretty common for prices to increase without anyone knowing. I don't expect to be notified whenever the price of my favorite jeans or restaurant entrée increases. Consumers understand that product prices are bound to change. No forewarning or apology is necessary to explain why the increase took place. It is what it is.

I see the photography industry in the same way. There is no need to warn all past clients every single time you increase prices. In fact, it can work against you. If you notify people of a price increase at a time when they weren't planning on hiring you, they're less likely to look at your website when they *do* have need of your services. It is better for clients to keep you in mind as "their" photographer. When they are ready to hire you again, they'll see the new pricing and choose whether to accept it or take a chance on another photographer. Deciding you no longer want to hire someone is easy when you don't currently have a need for that person's service. It is much harder for clients to walk away from increased pricing when there *is* a pressing need, such as getting holiday cards done.

Handle price increases by including a bit of copy on your website that lets clients know prices are subject to change at any time, and only booking a session will secure current pricing. You can also include a similar blurb in your contract or welcome packet if you feel the need to keep clients from memorizing your pricing.

If you want to reach out to past clients about the increase, combine the news with a taste of other changes that you are making to bring more luxury and a boutique experience to your services. Send your past clients a thank-you note for helping you build your business to what it is today, for instance. Let them know that you are making huge changes in your business to better serve the needs of your clients and so your rates will be increasing. Offer them the opportunity to book now with your current pricing.

If you offer clients a chance to book now at current rates before prices increase, give incentives, such as a $100 gift certificate to apply to their à la carte order, not discounts. Later, you can send out a mailing promoting your new launch prices and offering transition discounts for bookings before a specified date. Yes, send a physical mailing rather than an e-mail or a Facebook post. Marketing e-mails easily go unread, and Facebook rarely shows in feeds anymore. Look at ways to connect in a personal way with your past clients if you want to notify them of the increase, and you're more likely to get them to move forward with you.

When is the best time to raise my prices?

I hate to be the bearer of bad tidings, but there just never is a perfect time to raise prices. You can wait and wait for the perfect moment, but it's never going to come. Fortunately, there are signs that a price increase would be wise, so you'll know when the time is ripe for an adjustment:

- You aren't paying yourself a paycheck because there isn't money left over after expenses.
- You seem to be attracting people who hire you but still balk at your pricing—right in front of you.
- You want to work less but can't afford to reduce the amount of money you are currently bringing in.
- It's been more than two years since your last price increase.
- It's time for you to grow your business and hire an assistant to help reduce your workload.
- All your photographer friends are telling you to raise your prices because you are worth more.
- Your spouse is telling you to raise your prices because you are worth more.
- Your children are asking for quilted toilet paper instead of single ply.
- The IRS is telling you that your deductions exceed your income.

Despite these warning signs, you may never feel ready to raise your prices.

That wave of nausea may not pass until you get hired for the first time on that new pricing. You may constantly question yourself and doubt what you know you need to be doing. It's a terrifying thing to take a leap of faith and hope that you are making the right decision. But it's never the right decision to do nothing, to settle for what you know you are choosing to do because it's safe.

The only way to have long-term business success is to do what everyone else is afraid of doing. *That's* how to stand out. *That* is how you create an amazing business that is profitable and sustainable, one that your clients are thrilled to be part of because they know that you are in it for the long haul.

Other photographers ask to see my price list all the time. What do I do?

It's frustrating that after putting time and energy into creating the perfect pricing, you find that other photographers start asking to see your pricing. Sometimes they are up front and honest in asking for it, clear on their intentions of wanting to see it to help them build theirs. Others are sneaky about it, pretending to be a potential client to get their eyes on the prize. Either way, it's kind of annoying.

I wish I could get back the hours I used to waste researching if each person who e-mailed me as a potential client asking to see my price list was actually a potential client or a sneaky photographer. It was a pain because I found a higher percentage of photographers than actual clients. I felt like I had to sacrifice my valuable time trying to not accommodate dishonest people.

To handle this little nuisance, set your basic information on your website. All the basic information that any client needs to know should be found there, along with a contact number for those with less basic questions. This simple step completely eliminated tire kickers e-mailing me. If a photographer who was clear on his intentions were to contact me, I'd send him my price list—yep, even if he was a local competitor.

Because I put so much intentional strategy into creating my pricing (just as you will after reading this book), those prices are a reflection of my business acumen, my financial needs, and my self-confidence. An unethical competitor can steal the numbers, but not the intention and strategy. If he doesn't understand the method, the strategy, or the reasoning behind why the pricing is what it is, the pricing won't work for him.

For example, your competitor might balk at your price for canvases and slash it to be closer to his print prices. Then, he might get queasy at the collection prices, tweaking them and throwing in a few extra prints here and there to make them more "sellable." By the time he finishes making *your* pricing comfortable for him, it won't remotely resemble yours. The strategy will be completely gone. Even if someone copies and pastes your exact pricing, don't assume it's going to be the same success for him as it is for you. You *know* why your pricing is what it is. You are convinced that it has to be the way it is for a reason.

If sharing your price list makes you feel yucky, however, by all means, don't do it. Success doesn't come easily, and those who are serious about business will eventually find that out on their own—with or without your fab price list.

No matter what, my clients balk at my prices. What am I missing?

Every photographer dreads the client who can't contain her shock at seeing the price list. If you aren't completely confident in your pricing, that client's shock can make you question everything you are doing with your business. Worse, it can make you question who you are as a business person: "Do I really suck, and am I priced too high? Do they hate the way I'm dressed? Should I just quit now and forget ever getting beyond giving away what I do? Should I have used more psychology in my pricing, leaving off dollar signs or pricing the items in a certain order? Why do they keep looking at me that way?"

There are three simple reasons a client balks at pricing:

- She might just be a cheapie who expects far more than she is willing to pay.
- Her reaction is simply a sales objection.
- She is surprised by the information, which means you probably aren't presenting your pricing correctly.

No matter what you do or what your price point, you will always face someone who balks. The best way to reduce the number of clients who react this way (or the number you have to witness face to face, at least) is to make sure you are talking comfortably about your pricing in several different ways while you are communicating your services to clients. Be up front and honest at all times when addressing your pricing. I've seen far too many photographers do bait-and-switch pricing, offering a cheap session fee but then ridiculously high-priced prints. Although they may get hired, they don't retain their clients. We are going for clients who stick with us for the long haul!

To reduce the chances of facing those surprised-at-pricing client stares, put basic pricing, including your session fee, on your website. Prevent people from asking "Does that include a disc of the images?" by stating exactly what the session fee covers. No need to make it flowery; just tell them what to expect.

When whipping up your website's pricing information, also consider including the following:

- Starting size and price for prints
- Starting price for collections
- Your minimum order requirement
- Amount the average client spends

The last point is optional. If you are currently happy with your average sale, share it. (It works well for me!) If you'd rather not put your average sale out there, don't share. No biggie. Just don't falsify the information; skip it instead.

Finally, when a potential client calls, make sure you ask her if she has seen your basic pricing information on your website. If she hasn't, tell her right then and there what it is.

The more confident and comfortable you are with talking about your pricing, the more your client can trust you. There is no more uncomfortable feeling than talking to a professional who only alludes to vague pricing but never comes out and says what it is.

If saying your pricing out loud makes you want to dry heave, you've just plain got to get over it if you want your business to move on and grow. Be honest with yourself: Is the problem that your pricing isn't what it should be, or are you afraid of the unknown? Do not let the fear of the unknown ruin your ability to do something incredibly amazing with your business. You'll regret if for a lifetime.

Is it possible to have a business in a tiny town?

Yes! You can have a sustainable business in a small town because more often than not, small towns aren't overrun with photographers. Furthermore, small towns usually have the benefit of not having to compete with bargain-priced chain studios.

Metropolitan areas probably have a higher ratio of photographers to potential clients than small towns simply because everyone looks at the potential and sees themselves being surrounded by thousands or hundreds of thousands of potential clients.

True, a small town may have only a few thousand people from which to draw a client base, but once you do your homework from previous chapters, you may discover that you need only a small number of clients to stay in business. You don't need thousands of clients per year to have a profitable and sustainable business unless you are a $50 shoot-and-burn photographer. With the right pricing and the right marketing, you need to attract only a few dozen per year. That's totally doable.

Better yet, word-of-mouth spreads like wildfire in small towns, which means easier marketing because it's easier to circulate your reputation. Friends will talk to friends, and your marketing gets a whole lot easier. You also have the ability to work with local businesses because you have the chance to get to know them better. This is your chance to really step up and bring a community together in supporting small businesses. When small-business owners unite, everyone in the community feels the positive effects. There is a lot of creative marketing just waiting to happen right there!

Even if you already have a photographer or two doing business in your town, you probably know them and all about their reputations. You're better able to set yourself apart as something very different. This makes you less threatening to existing businesses, and it allows you to see the niche you can carve out for yourself with laser focus. If an established local photographer shoots everything from weddings to seniors to high-school pictures to passport pictures, find something that you do extremely well that perhaps your competitor doesn't do so well and heavily market yourself for that. Become the photographer who doesn't compete with the other locals, just the one who fills in the gaps where the others are weak.

Be creative and show your community something new. In a small community, your style can stand out and shine because you aren't like anyone else. Seize that opportunity, and run wild with it! Refuse to be discouraged because you live in a small town. You can totally do it with a clearly defined style, other local businesses, and relational marketing.

How am I ever going to be sustainable and compete with photographers offering $75 sessions that include a disc?

The minute you enter the photography industry in any sort of serious manner, you become aware of the multitude of ridiculously cheap photographers out there. They seem to be everywhere, don't they?

Pay them no attention, and do not dread their presence!

Finding a dozen photographers in your neighborhood who are dirt cheap doesn't necessarily mean that they are going to stay that cheap. This could be a phase for them; perhaps some are just starting out or are hobbyists at heart. Most likely, they will either burn out or get a clue that a sustainable business can't go on like this. Things will change one way or another. Give them time to see the light, but don't waste any time worrying about their effect on your business.

Not everyone wants to hire a beginner or the most dirt-cheap offering that they can. Just as some people value $200 photographers but might not a $2000 option, other people value $750 photographers but not $75. There truly are people out there who hire based on style and not ultimately on price. Look for those people, market to them, and use your pricing to attract them.

When I had my studio in Montana, I can't tell you how many times I was told that I was hired *because* I was the highest-priced photographer in the state. Hiring me wasn't about clients just wanting to blow money; it was about getting what they paid for. Clients had the most confidence in me because I had the most confidence in myself to present the highest pricing. I didn't try to be competitive with everyone else around me by keeping it cheap and safe. It also took me years to get to that point, so don't expect to just put out a price list and assume because you are higher than everyone it's going to work for you. You still have to earn the reputation that can back up that pricing!

Those cheap-as-dirt photographers won't be able to compete with you because you are going to offer better customer service and a better customer experience. That's going to help retain your clients and not lose them to the cheaper photographers.

Focus your business energy on *why* you have your pricing and *why* it's worthwhile for clients to pony up the cash. Assuming you followed the advice in this book, your pricing is a product of common sense, sound judgment, real need, and compensation for your time and talent.

Finally, remember that no matter what price range you're in, you're going to be in competition with other photographers at that price point. Let the competition be good for your business instead of letting it anger or discourage you. Keep growing and work to get to the ultimate place of competition: outdoing *yourself*. That's when you'll really shine.

How should I approach portfolio building?

I once received a vendor e-mail invitingly titled, "We want to feature you!" The body of the message then went on to explain the cost I had to pay to be featured. It made me feel gross all over knowing that the business didn't really want to feature me so much as to make money while making itself look good. This bait-and-switch tactic is just sleazy marketing, and it's a lot like a photographer offering free portfolio-building sessions as a way to attract potential sales.

When I was first starting out, I learned the "Fresh Faces" marketing method from a photographer. Her advice was to print and hand out hundreds of cards offering potential models free photo sessions and a complimentary 8×10 as a thank-you gift. It was her highly recommended method of not only filling your portfolio and gaining a new client, but also of making sales after the session. I was new; she made money, and she held workshops. Why shouldn't I trust her and give it a try?

I printed 500 oversize postcards and littered the community with them. Although I did fill my portfolio quickly with a ton of these free sessions, it was an exhausting and expensive learning process. I spent hundreds of hours driving, shooting, and editing on top of a large hunk of money on the marketing materials and the complimentary 8×10 prints I gave out. I gave away 30 sessions in a month, and only three actually placed an order. I made a grand total of less than $150, which didn't even cover my expenses. Guess how many clients hired me again? None, zero, zip. All of that work toward marketing and sales, and all I got was a portfolio and a lot of valuable lessons on how *not* to run a business.

If you are requesting models to photograph for your portfolio that results in *you* looking better, then do not charge them *at all*. Hand over the discs of their images, and thank the models for helping and benefitting you. Don't use this as an underhanded method to get orders.

I believe there is a time and place for free sessions, but I do not believe that time is ever when the goal is to grow a client base or attract potential sales. If you want to build a client base and you're over getting your feet wet, you've got to charge! Otherwise, you're bait-and-switching, and that's no good.

Is custom framing worth adding to my line of offerings? How do I charge for it?

As you remember from Chapter 2, "Your Ideal Client & Marketplace," I am not a proponent of carrying custom frames. The main reason why is that their high cost of good makes profitability difficult.

Remember as well that you should mark up specialty items by at least five times your cost of goods as a bare minimum. You must always leave some wiggle room to make a profit on a product so that you can sell it at a discount (as in your collections) or offer it as an incentive (to entice larger sales).

Why the wiggle room? Consider some numbers. If a product costs you $50 and you charge $250 (five times the cost) for it, you make $200 each time it sells. But if your client purchases it using one of your promotions or discounts (say, 25 percent off), he gets the product for $187.50. That leaves you a profit of just $137.50, which is still not too bad. A markup of two times the cost means a profit of only $50 on the regular price ($100) and a mere $25 on the discounted price ($75)—bad for profitability.

Of course, if you want to sell frames, you have to consider more than the cost of the frame and print. You also have to purchase corner samples from the framing company, sample frames, and perhaps mounting supplies, all of which add to the cost, not to mention factoring in the value of your time, if you're brave enough to try mounting prints yourself. Those "extra" costs add up very quickly without getting you much bang for your buck.

Now compare selling your gift prints to selling a specialty item like custom framing. If your gift print price is $50 and your client has $250 to spend, he can choose five 8×10s (total COGS about $15) or he can choose your specialty item for $250 (COGS $50). Not only does selling the 8×10s mean you profit more, it also means your client gets more bang for his buck—you both win.

As you can see, specialty items with a high cost of goods sold, like custom frames, aren't as profitable as you might imagine. If that doesn't stop you cold in your tracks, perhaps exploding a couple myths will:

- Offering custom framing will *not* increase sales. If a client has a $2000 budget, offering custom framing is not going to get him to spend over that budget. It will merely cut into your print sales by increasing frame sales. Increasing sales is beneficial only if you increase profits at the same time. It's better to have a $500 sale with 50 cost of goods ($450 profit) than it is to have a $1000 sale with $600 cost of goods ($400 profit).

- Offering a framed product that is ready to hang will *not* increase orders for larger prints. If someone isn't a fan of or doesn't have room for large prints, he isn't going to change because of your line of custom frames. One of my biggest clients never ordered larger than an 8×10, but the person's orders often totaled more than $2000. I could not convince that client to go bigger, no matter what angle I took. If you want to offer a ready-to-hang product, push the gallery-wrapped canvas choices you offer—which results in a higher profit to you and the client doesn't have to set aside a mental budget to pay a custom framer.

If a client is dead-set on custom framing, here is your opportunity to collaborate with a local framing company. Suggest the company offer a small discount in the form of a "5 percent to 10 percent off" coupon that you could give to all of your clients when you refer them to the framer. Keep an example of some of the framer's pricing on hand at your ordering sessions so you can give clients a rough estimate of the cost of framing, as well. Your clients will appreciate you looking out for them and helping them to decide their the best option—and you won't have to buy a single frame corner.

Other photographers around me are so successful; how can I compete while building my new business?

You have to open yourself to failure.

I have had to learn this lesson the hard way: by failing miserably more than I have ever succeeded naturally and effortlessly. I'm willing to admit my failures, find my errors, and help others prevent making the same mistakes that I once made. That's right, I'm only successful because I have been a huge failure.

Still, I continue to do things that are total flops, but typically (and thankfully), no one is the wiser, which is just the thing: Everybody struggles, but we don't always see it.

You don't know when your competitors are failing. You only see them succeeding. Maybe it took your top competitor 15 marketing promotions to get 10 clients, but you see only those 10 clients and assume her road to being all booked up was effortless.

Just because your competition or the others surrounding you in the industry are coming off as incredibly successful doesn't mean they don't struggle. Don't be so quick to put them on a pedestal or minimize their efforts. You have no idea what it took for them to get to that place or even what is currently going on in their lives. They may have money to buy things you are dying for, but you don't know what they are sacrificing to get it. They may have tons of clients, but you don't really know how much money they are making and if all their clients love what they do.

Nobody is perfect, and nobody has it easy. You just don't:

- Hear their horror stories.
- See the times that they mess things up.
- Hear about the clients that are beasts. (Yes, even the most successful business people attract beasts for clients sometimes.)

The only person you should be competing with to build your business is *you*, so ask yourself these questions:

- Have I done all I can for today? (*Really*?)
- Have I stuck to my marketing calendar or my business plan?
- Have I taken care of my clients to the best of my abilities?
- Have I put one foot in front of the other and been open to failure?

Those are the benchmarks of a growing entrepreneur, and the sooner you learn to do your own thing to the best of your ability, using only *your* actions as the steps to success, the better off you'll be.

My clients push their time limits for scheduling and ordering during the holiday season. How can I prevent this?

During my first year of business, I gave my clients no boundaries, expectations, or deadlines, which left me scrambling to deliver orders as late as December 23. The following year, things changed.

In early autumn I posted a holiday-season schedule on my website, listing the dates that I had available and the session fee for those dates. October dates listed my usual session fee and minimum order requirement (MOR). For November dates, I bumped up my session fee by 25 percent and my MOR by 20 percent, meaning my session fee increased from $200 to $250 and my MOR from $500 to $600. During the last week of November and first week of December clients are really pushing the limit time-wise, so I increased the rates for those dates by 50 percent for my session fee ($300) and 30 percent for my MOR ($700). The truly time-challenged could book "Last Minute Holiday Sessions" during the second and third weeks of December at *double* my usual rates: a session fee of $400 and MOR of $1000. Boy, did that motivate people to book early!

To apply this strategy to your business and get your holiday bookings in earlier, follow these steps:

1. **Pick your dates**: Identify the period during which you want people to book holiday sessions, and keep those dates at your regular session and MOR prices. Choose the dates on which you will be willing to shoot but will treat the sessions as a quick turnaround; raise your session and MOR rates accordingly. (You may choose to price these dates as a single increase or break them into two pricing tiers as I did.) Lastly, pick the dates on which you will be willing to shoot but would rather spend eating pie at holiday parties, and charge double your rates during this time. If clients are procrastinators or really desperate, you can still squeeze them in, but on *your* terms. Once clients know delay comes at a cost, they'll make more effort to book early.
2. **Communicate your new holiday pricing policy**: As I did, post your holiday schedule on your website well in advance. As a courtesy, e-mail your price schedule and available dates to your client list to give your old clients fair warning that waiting until the last minute will come at a cost this year.
3. **Provide a set of guidelines for ordering**: Clearly state that if clients place an order within three to four days of receiving their galleries or before a specific date (say, November 15), it's business as usual. After that date, *all* orders will be considered rush orders. Rush orders come with faster turnarounds, less time to place the order, and an extra cost for rush printing. Keep the clients moving so that not for a minute are they going to slack on placing their order. Be clear that delaying decision making literally costs money, so they'll follow the deadlines.
4. **Reward your clients for completing orders on time**: Give clients a personal gift as a thank-you for making your holiday season a little less stressful, or you could surprise them with a few additional prints or a gorgeous calendar.

No matter the schedule you choose, communicate it thoroughly and clearly up front and then thank clients for abiding by it. The more pleasant the overall experience, the more likely clients will return next year and perhaps even book sooner.

People love me when I shoot for free, but as soon as I start charging, they disappear. Am I not worth my prices?

One of the best and most encouraging pieces of advice I have ever received came from my first business coach, Naomi Dunford of IttyBiz: "The easiest way to sell things is to present them to people who have some interest in buying them. Get rid of the nonbuyers now, and they won't be a pain in your ass later."

That's right, every time someone runs for the hills when you present your pricing, be grateful. It is nothing personal. These people never intended to give you their money, and now you know. There is no need to waste your time and energy marketing to a group of people who have no intention of ever hiring you.

Let's face it, people love free things. The minute you remind them that you are in the business of making money and that your mission is not really to lessen the financial load of everyone that you come in contact with by never charging anything for your services, they bolt. They just don't want to part with their money.

When you're building your business and establishing your new, well-researched, and planned pricing, it may seem like everyone is out to take advantage of you. They'll take free but not pay. Hang in there.

There *are* people who are willing to part with their money for your services. Keep marketing, keep looking, and don't give up on humanity entirely.

When people run for the hills, you are refining your client list. You are finding people who have the capacity to be genuine clients soon or at some point in the future. You are weeding out the people who like to ride the free train and finding people who want to ride the pay train. That, my friends, is golden.

Is it really possible to go from new to booming quickly?

Happily, I can say from personal experience that it *is* possible to go from new to booming quickly. From starting out a new business to having a steady flow of midrange-priced clients (spending more than $1500) took me less than a year, and then the second year my sales increased from midrange to high end (clients spending more than $3000). It was difficult but not impossible.

If you have the option of growing slowly and steadily, I encourage you to take that path. The new-to-booming path can be overwhelming, and more often than not, it's growth through trial and error instead of being educated, simply because there isn't much time to learn and develop the business side.

If you need a business and need it soon, here are three lessons that put me on the fast track to business growth:

- **Keep growing your pricing**: I did almost monthly price raises the first year to get myself into a place of securing higher sales. It was painful because each price increase eliminated the clients from the previous price group, but it had to be done to finally secure the price group that I needed my business to be in.
- **Put lots of eggs in your relational marketing basket**: I was rubbing shoulders any and every way I could think of with other business owners in the area. I shopped for a lot of session props and referred clients for purchasing session outfits to one particular children's boutique, and I ended up doing mini-sessions there. My client base was established through the store's mailing list and advertising of those mini-sessions. If I hadn't stepped out of my comfort zone to build a relationship with the store owner, she would have never asked me to do the sessions, which became an annual event.
- **Be open to failure**: I tried a lot of things that were major bombs. Out of each experiment, however, I learned something new and often gained a new client who ended up becoming a future referrer.

Not everything you do is going to seem profitable or may even look like it's working from the start. It takes a lot of patience to wait for your marketing efforts to really sink in for some people. Photography isn't an impulse buy, although we as photographers love to think that it is. For some people, it may take a year or two years to hire you after your marketing efforts.

If things aren't booming, look for ways that you can grow right where you are while you wait for business to pick up. You can't just sit refreshing your inbox waiting for inquiries. You need to evaluate your pricing (remember, too low can turn off people as much as too high can), your relational marketing efforts, and your willingness to experiment with new promotions and ideas.

Is this photography market *really* sustainable?

Since the invention of digital photography and user-friendly Adobe Photoshop, substantially more new photographers are in the industry compared to 20 years ago. I'll wager that the rate of people getting out of the market is growing also. More importantly, I believe that the *demand* for photography has grown.

Custom photography is more accessible than it once was, because there are more photographers available to do it. Instead of scheduling a family photo session at a local studio once every few years, families do so much more regularly. With online sharing, the demand for photography is like never before. So naturally, there is an increase in photographers.

Whether the market is sustainable largely depends on which market you are in and how much work you are willing to put into it. The shoot-and-burn market will always be there, for example, as will clients who want what they want for as cheaply as they can possibly get it. Can a single photographer thrive in this market? Although I could work in this market if necessity demanded it of me, I personally wouldn't survive long because I do not have the desire for a high-volume business lifestyle. That market isn't sustainable for me, *but* it could last for someone who enjoys high-volume, low-effort photography and doesn't have a lifestyle that requires higher sales. I've seen photographers who have been doing this for decades, and it's sustainable for them.

I believe the real issue lies with the number of new photographers who come into the photography business thinking that it's going to be easy money with little effort or expense. A large percentage of photographers enter the industry with nothing but a camera, an empty bank account, and a whole lot of entitlement issues. In my opinion, they aren't preventing the market from being sustainable because they don't last long. In the three to six months it takes to find out that being an business owner (whether you are a photographer or a pie maker) is not easy money, those individuals give up. They find that a business will not sustain itself without a substantial investment of time, money, energy, or all three.

Is the market sustainable? Yes, if you're one of those talented people willing to invest time and energy into creating business success in the longer term. Those who want to enter the business, undercut pricing, and "get rich quick" aren't creating a sustainable business, however, they'll be gone in a few months.

Should I offer in-person or online ordering?

Sitting down with a client one-on-one for an ordering session certainly has the potential for bigger sales. During the three years I had my studio in Montana, for example, I did online ordering primarily. I tried in-person ordering with a handful of clients and my sales were higher because I coached them to buy several products that they wouldn't have thought to add to their cart on their own. If I'd followed that approach regularly, I probably would have consistently doubled my online sales or better.

Despite that, I chose to stick with online ordering because it worked best for my family during that season of our lives. My time out of the home was limited, and I had to keep that time strictly to shooting. Also, the times that I would have been able to meet with clients just were not at reasonable hours. Who wants to have an ordering session at 11:30 at night?

note I used Photo Cart for my online ordering. Although PicturesPro still sells Photo Cart, the company has ceased developing for it and, instead, is putting its energies into Sytist, which is a similar but more elaborate system.

I found a system that worked consistently for me. Using software from PicturesPro (www.picturespro.com), I was able to create packages and use minimum order requirements with my clients that gave me a consistent sale. My clients seemed content with the method, and they knew I was available to chat by phone if they needed help with the process. I was thorough about explaining the collections and other choices, as well as the ordering process. It was a breeze for them, and everyone was happy.

At that time, the higher sales and added profit from in-person sales would have been great, but to me they weren't worth the trade-off of the hours I would need to invest to achieve them. Choose a system that works best for your current life, but remember, the season of your life may change. You may bounce between online and in-person sales over the years, which is fine. If you have the time and look forward to the relationship-building side of your business, in-person sales may be a good fit. If you can't spare any more minutes from family or other commitments, online sales may be the better choice. It's your call!

How do I sell more using online galleries?

Although I averaged $2000 and more with my online sales, that's rare. The keys to my success were constant refinement and hyper-vigilance. The foundation of it was to post all client galleries online for four days. That amount of time is not random. Considering most portrait studios get away with instant in-person ordering after a photo shoot, four days to mull over a decision is incredibly generous. The biggest mistake photographers make with online ordering is to leave client galleries up for long periods with no end date in sight. A deadline concentrates the mind; give clients four days, no more.

To make sure those four days are successful, follow these hyper-vigilant steps:

1. **When a client is on the phone to finalize the booking for the session, clearly outline the process after the session**: Keep it simple; don't overwhelm with too many details. Do cover basic information, and be sure to state the time frames that you will be working with so that the client has an realistic expectations and understands that you have a system. Your business has policies that are in place to ensure profitability. If you have been lax on enforcing your policies, stop. You want to have a high-end business, so treat it as such. Your clients are important, and their expectations are just as important.

   For me, a typical call goes something like this: "After your session, I will post sneak-peek images on my blog for you to see. Then, you will receive your online slideshow to view all your images within four to six days. You will also receive access information to your online ordering gallery with your slideshow. You will have four days to place your order, and during this time, never hesitate to call or e-mail me if you need any help."

tip The faster you turn around your images for your clients, the happier they'll be! They may resent having only four days if you take twice that or longer to post the gallery.

2. **Get a signed contract before you begin shooting**: That's right, *before* you even start shooting, whip out your policies for them to sign. I prefer doing this in person instead of through the mail, because I can use the meeting to briefly run over a few points that I want to emphasize.

   This is another chance to remind clients that they will have four days to place a portrait order. This time, include in your contract your policies about the fee involved for republishing their gallery if it expires. I also mention in my policies that after the gallery is republished, only à la carte pricing is available. (In other words, clients can no longer order collections and take advantage of their savings.) Encourage your clients in every way possible to order during your designated time frame. Make sure they're paying attention when you say these things!

3. **Remind clients of the time frame after the portrait session ends and confirm the deadline for orders**: When wrapping up, for instance, I again tell the client something like, "Alright! Tomorrow, I will have a blog post up for you so that you can get a sneak peek of the session. Then on Monday, the 4th, you will receive an e-mail from me that will include the link to your slideshow as well as your online ordering information. You then will have four days to place your order. Will you be able to finalize your order by the evening of Thursday the 7th? Or, is there a better four-day time frame for you?"

This dialogue shows clients that you are firm on time frames, but you can be flexible to find what works best for their schedule. The client has the opportunity to tell you that Wednesday would be better or next week is ideal. At the same time, the client is agreeing to place the order in four days because you accommodated his schedule.

tip Clients love sneak peeks because they provide peace of mind that the session went well. The waiting time between session and receiving the ordering gallery will be a lot more bearable for them, too.

4. **Blog a sneak peek and remind the clients of the time frame once again**: The day after the session, e-mail your client to say that the blog post is up (include a link to the post). Also call him to let him know you sent the e-mail and thank him for hiring you to photograph his family. At the same time, take the opportunity to reassure your client that he is going to love the images that you captured and let him know how excited you are for him to see them. Remind the client of the day and date that he will be hearing from you again with the slideshow and online ordering gallery.
5. **Prepare the online ordering gallery and notification e-mail the night before and then send it early in the morning of delivery day**: Some people wake up and go straight to their computers to check their e-mail. I love thrilling my clients by having news of their online galleries waiting for them in their inboxes because it goes above and beyond their expectations. Be sure the e-mail specifies the day and date that the ordering gallery will expire and reminds the client to contact you if he needs any help placing his order.
6. **Check in and make sure client questions are answered**: The day after you send the slideshow and ordering gallery, call or e-mail your client to ask whether he has any questions for you. (I usually do this during a time that I assume the person's voicemail will pick up.) Just check to make sure that the client received all the information and let the person know that you're available by phone or e-mail to answer questions any time before the deadline (restate the date, just in case).
7. **Remind one last time**: The day before the gallery expires, send the client another quick e-mail reminder that the gallery is about to expire. Remind him of the fee to republish the gallery and that collections will no longer be available after the expiration, only à la carte prices. Again, assure the person that you are there to help if he needs it.

Step 8 is up to the client: place the order. But what if he doesn't? Face it, some clients will just take forever and money is no object. I have had one client that always lets her gallery expire—usually at least three times. She pays the republishing fee and à la carte prices without blinking.

When dealing with your own procrastinators, be firm about your policies. Make sure that you collect the republishing fee up front before you activate the gallery. I always do this over the phone by taking a credit card number. These clients have no one to be upset with but themselves. (Remember that!) During the call, remind the client that he has again just four more days in which to order.

If a client comes to you with a sob story or a horror story of why they couldn't place the order, look at it case by case. The wonderful thing about policies is that they are there for your protection. Sometimes clients have legitimate reasons why they couldn't order on time, and this is your opportunity to give them even more excellent customer service by asking, "Would an extra two days help? Would it be better if I waited to publish the gallery in the next week for four days?" I always lead with what I'm willing to do and what would work best for my business. I don't ask open-ended questions like, "How much time do you need? When would you like this?"

You are the business, you are in charge. Be flexible, be understanding. But be profitable, too!

All my friends and family want sessions. What do I charge?

My method for handling friends and family is simple: super-close family members and friends who I adore get the session and images totally free. I shoot the sessions at a time that's convenient for me and ask them to be flexible. I don't bother with online galleries, slideshows, or blog posts—just a few hours of time and simple edits.

Friends of friends and people who I wouldn't run into a burning building to rescue receive a flat session fee that includes the digital files, understanding that client work and client orders have priority over their session processing and delivery—again, no online galleries, slideshows, or blog posts.

If any of my family members or friends want to be treated like a client, meaning they require specific days, have special requests for the session, want to order prints, or want retouching services, then they pay full price, just like a client, with no discount. If family members want the time and energy a client takes, they become a client. They get the welcome packet, the cute mailing, the reminder phone calls, the slideshow, the blog post, the gallery, and the perfect packaging, and they pay for all of it.

I present both options to the loved one or friend when asked for a session, saying something like "Sure, I'd love to have a session with you! I can do it totally free for you by fitting you in the next time I have an available slot, so long as you're willing to be flexible in case a client ends up booking. You'll get a CD of edited images a few weeks after the session. Or, you can hire me, book a final date right now, and have the full client treatment at full price. Your choice." This way, I don't end up resenting friends and family sessions.

I posted my new pricing, but no one is calling. What now?

Don't give up on your all new pricing just yet. I know how terrifying it can be to present a whole new price list, especially if it's an increase. When the phone doesn't ring, you're sure that you've killed your business. You're thinking of selling your props on eBay or to that new photographer down the street. You're desperate enough to consider shooting those pictures of your son's T-ball team for the "exposure" and nothing else!

Before you turn to eBay for income or to telling four-year-olds how to hold their bats, consider that new pricing often means attracting a whole new group of clients, so it's natural that your business will slow down for a time. Even if you are fortunate enough to bring some of your clients forward from the old pricing, you are going to need to attract a whole crowd of new ones. Simply putting your new price list out there is not enough to keep the steady flow of inquiries and bookings that you had going before. If you already had a slow business, it's going to get even slower. If you were crazy busy, you'll probably become slow and steady.

But don't fret! It's not just you; this happens to everyone in business. Whether you've been around for 30 days or 30 years, people don't respond well to raised prices. It takes time for clients to find you.

Instead of staring at your inbox waiting for people to send you inquiries, use this time to focus on your marketing efforts and start making connections. Whether that's partnering with local businesses to create events, starting mail campaigns, revving up word-of-mouth with booking incentives, or creating in-store displays where the target clients for your new pricing shop, marketing is an active word that needs to be the cornerstone of your business for the next few months.

Keep at it. Just like putting out new pricing, marketing requires some patience, as well. As long as you keep growing your reach, you will eventually bring those new people in. And once you do, those clients will start doing word-of-mouth marketing for you. And *then*, those trips to your inbox may be a whole lot more productive.

What if a client asks for a discount?

I try to discourage discounts as much as possible because the client wins, but your bank account loses. For instance, suppose you have a minimum order requirement of $400. To get new clients in the door, you try offering 20 percent off all purchases. When clients spend the minimum, that discount means you get only a $320 sale. They client saved $80, you lost $80, and your minimum was not met.

As a better alternative, try incentives and bonuses. Get your clients to meet you at the price point *you* determine and then reward them for doing so. For example, offer a $100 print credit to clients spending $400. You get your minimum, and clients get a "free" $100 worth of prints!

Don't forget that discounts bring out the cheapness in people, and you may not be attracting your target market if clients aren't willing to pay full price. Instead, keep your target market happy by giving incentives worth talking about.

My clients constantly make special requests. How do I respond to them?

Special requests can be quite profitable, when handled correctly. The best solution depends on the type of request:

- **Last-minute sessions**: Some clients are insistent on earlier dates for sessions than what's available. If clients don't want to wait, offer to squeeze them into your calendar but explain the session fee will be $100 above the standard rate and that they are required to sign a collection purchase agreement. That's right, a client must commit to buying a collection in order to be bumped up in the queue. Believe me, everyone will be happy with the outcome!
- **Rush orders**: Some clients simply can't wait two weeks for their orders, and they're willing to pay to get them sooner. A 10 to 20 percent rush charge does wonders to distinguish between urgent needs and clients who are just being a bit high maintenance.
- **Booked dates**: If you have a client who simply must have a session date that's already booked, offer a happy compromise. Ask the scheduled client to change dates in exchange for a $250 print credit and then charge the incoming client $250 more for insisting upon the previously booked date. Most clients are simply thrilled to swap dates in the name of a fabulous print credit, and you've already made up the money with the incoming one!

note For a great perspective on rush jobs, see Seth Godin's blog post, "What to do with special requests" at http://sethgodin.typepad.com/seths_blog/2009/07/what-to-do-with-special-requests.html.

I'm thinking of offering a baby plan. What do you suggest?

When I started in business, I offered a $250 six-session baby plan that included sessions during pregnancy, of the newborn, and at the three-month, six-month, nine-month, and one-year marks. Each session came with a complimentary 8×10 and a spiral-bound proof book. I soon realized that I was giving away too much stuff and that clients were coming to me for their sessions, taking the freebies, and not ordering. I was booked a few months in advance, but these zero-dollar-spenders were taking up prime spots on the calendar.

So, I changed my baby plan to $300 for newborn, six-month, and one-year sessions and tossed in 10 percent off each session order. At the time, my MOR was $300. Clients spent about $400 to $600 on the first session and then just barely met the minimum with the remaining two. Not only were they budgeting their current orders based on how much they were going to spend for the rest of the year, they were also more hesitant to buy larger images or too many, in case the next session was even better.

Eventually, I dropped the baby plan altogether. I realized that if parents really loved my work, they would come back to me again at those milestone ages. This may be true for your business, too.

If you are convinced a baby plan is best for your business, however, don't let anyone else's negative experience (even mine) stop you. Here are some tips to help you keep baby plans profitable and the sessions enjoyable:

- If you do a maternity session, combine the maternity order together with the client's newborn order. This eliminates the all-too-common maternity order of only two 5×7 prints and saves you time and lab costs.
- Consider incentives carefully. Encourage clients to "spend more to save more" instead of giving out freebies. For every $500 spent offer an additional $100 print credit, for instance; or offer one complimentary digital file for every $300 spent! When you put incentives in place, make sure they maximize sales, not kill them!
- Make darn sure you enjoy photographing the ages for which you're booking sessions. I realized very quickly that I didn't enjoy blobby three-month-olds and tippy six-month-olds. My favorites were newborns and babies at nine months, yet the plan I offered forced me to work with the ages that I didn't enjoy in order to get the opportunity to photograph those that I did. It was draining, my heart wasn't in it, and the images betrayed that secret.

- Keep in mind that the clients you book will be with you for an *entire year*. If the parent is an awesome client, the year will be wonderful! If a client is high maintenance and not the best fit for your business, however, you'll be regretting taking the job for a long time.

Help beyond pricing

Profitability doesn't simply just start at pricing and end there. Your profitability is determined by so much more: the type of clients you work with, how you market, how you sell, how you manage your finances, how you get people to continually return, how you perform your customer service, how you manage your time, and more. The sections that follow point you toward finding help on all those other issues: marketing, branding, client communication, website copy, time management, overspending, financial mismanagement. I've included some of my favorite resources, organized by the chapters to which they're most relevant, so you can further your knowledge. I hope that these resources help you continue growing your business in profitability like they have for me!

Chapter 1 additional resources

Creating a realistic business budget can be challenging. Most entrepreneurs would rather figure out how to work with what they *get* instead of trying to figure out what they actually *need* for their businesses to produce based on how much their personal needs require. If a second income provides money into your household, figuring out your business budget can be even more difficult.

The best way to look at your business budget and its financial needs is to look at it as if you didn't have any other income coming in. What would you need to produce to cover *all* of your expenses to keep your business operational? That number is where you will find your business expenses, which would include the things that most small-business owners skip over because they are also using that thing for personal purposes, such as a phone, Internet connection, and so on. If your business uses it and you didn't have a second income to pay for it, that is now a business expense. Treating it that way immediately will quickly train you to have a realistic view of your business operational expenses so that if your second income goes away, your business will already be prepared to cover those expenses. The motivation to make more money will be stronger when you remove the second income as a backup resource. Profitability comes when you are realistic with your numbers with what your business is producing as well as covering!

When you are creating your business budget goals with the gross earning calculator and you feel stuck on what numbers to start with, I recommend these books to figure out what you need for your business to produce based on a deeper understanding of your personal finances. In particular, if you need advice on financial management and money mind-sets, I recommend reading the following:

- *Small Business Financial Management Kit for Dummies* by Tage C. Tracy (For Dummies, 2007)
- *Let's Do This: An Entrepreneur's Guide to Knowing When to Quit Your Day Job* by AJ Johnston (AJ Johnston, 2015)
- *Overcoming Underearning: A Five Step Plan to a Richer Life* by Barbara Stanny (HarperBusiness, 2007)
- *Earn What Your Deserve: How To Stop Underearning and Start Thriving* by Jerrold Mundis (Random House, 1996)
- *MONEY Master the Game: 7 Simple Steps to Financial Freedom* by Tony Robbins (Simon & Schuster, 2014)

For advice on time management and scheduling, consider the following:

- *168 Hours: You Have More Time Than You Think* by Laura Vanderkam (Portfolio, 2010)
- *Manage Your Day-to-Day: Build Your Routine, Find Your Focus, and Sharpen Your Creative Mind* by Jocelyn K. Glei (Amazon Publishing, 2013)

In addition, the Paymo time-tracking app (www.paymoapp.com/time-tracking) can help you get more realistic numbers on how much time you are spending per client.

If you aren't ready to hire a full- or even part-time local assistant but need some extra help, a virtual assistant could be the answer. Natalie Sisson's article "7 Ways a Virtual Assistant Can Save You at Least Two Hours Each Day to Focus on Your Income Producing Activities" (http://suitcaseentrepreneur.com/mind-body-balance/7-ways-a-virtual-assistant-can-save-you-at-least-2-hours-each-day-to-focus-on-your-income-producing-activities/) offers excellent suggestions on how a virtual assistant can help your business. Where do you find one? Here are some of my favorite sites:

- Task Rabbit (United States, www.taskrabbit.com)
- Kutoto (Canada, www.kutoto.com)

- VA Networking (www.vanetworking.com/clients)
- Virtual Assistant Forum (www.virtualassistantforums.com/submit_job.php)

Don't forget to ask other photographers for recommendations, as well. You never know when a photographer needs extra work and might make a great virtual assistant who already understands the business operations!

Using an online project management system is another option to help you manage your business and your time more efficiently and reduce the overwhelm of having multiple processes and procedures. These are two good options:

- 17Hats Business Management Program (www.17hats.com)
- Asana Project Management (http://asana.com)

Have a tax question that you are struggling with as you go through your gross earning calculator? Many CPAs don't fully understand the sales model of photographers, but Amy Northard is a certified public accountant who focuses on the needs of creative professionals and understands the photography industry. If you need advice, you can contact her at http://amynorthardcpa.com.

Chapter 2 additional resources

The "Ideal Client" worksheets are some of the most challenging exercises in this book, but they're also the most powerful. Struggling photographers need to laser focus on their ideal, target clients and market instead of trying to be the photographer for everyone. When your pricing isn't working, your marketing isn't working. If you're still stuck on the worksheet or need to go back to the "Ideal Client" drawing board, here are some blog posts that may help:

- "How to Tell if Your Dream Customer Is Actually Dreamy?" (www.braidcreative.com/blog/how-to-tell-if-your-dream-customer-is-actually-dreamy)
- "What Creatives who Attract Dream Clients Do" (www.braidcreative.com/blog/what-creatives-who-attract-dream-clients-do)
- "How to Get Clear on Your Target Market and Never Have to Hunt for Your Next Gig Again" (www.themiddlefingerproject.org/how-to-get-clear-on-your-target-market-and-never-have-to-hunt-for-your-next-gig-again)

Hands-down, one of my favorite courses on branding to attract your best clients that are "your people" is Scott and Elise Grice's My Own Irresistible Brand at www.myownirresistiblebrand.com.

If you're not sure where you shine in the marketplace, these three books may help:

- *You Are a Badass: How to Stop Doubting Your Greatness and Start Living an Awesome Life* by Jen Sincero (Running Press, 2013)
- *The Pumpkin Plan: A Simple Strategy to Grow a Remarkable Business in Any Field* by Mike Michalowicz (Portfolio, 2012)
- *Riches in Niches: How to Make It Big in a Small Market* by Susan A. Friedman(Career Press, 2007)

If you'd rather listen than read it, try Brian Tracy's audio book *Selling Higher Priced Products Against Lower Priced Competition* (www.briantracy.com/catalog/selling-higher-priced-products-against-lower-priced-competition), which offers advice about selling luxury.

Chapter 3 additional resources

Because I always get asked who I recommend for printing, I've included some of my favorite printers who I have worked with. I don't have a single favorite because they all have their own valuable merits. I always recommend first checking to see whether you have a local printer. You may pay slightly more, but having a face-to-face relationship with the company that you are working with can be a valuable resource for networking as well. If keeping it local isn't an option or your usual printer can't handle specialty items, these online printers offer a range of services:

- www.artifactuprising.com
- www.whcc.com
- www.bayphoto.com
- www.millers.com
- www.adoramapix.com
- www.prodpi.com
- www.canvasondemand.com
- www.thefindlab.com

Chapter 4 additional resources

Once you have your pricing, your next challenge is going to be *selling* your work. Pricing doesn't stop with handing a price list to a client and asking what they want to buy. Your pricing is the most effective when you have a solid grasp on *how* you are selling and, most importantly, are selling to your clients' needs and desires. These books are all some of the best resources I have come across to help you find your own unique style of selling to your ideal client:

- *Selling Luxury: Connect with Affluent Customers, Create Unique Experiences Through Impeccable Service, and Close the Sale* by Robin Lent and Geneviève Tour (Wiley, 2009)
- *Little Red Book of Selling: 12.5 Principles of Sales Greatness* by Jeffrey Gitomer (Bard Press, 2004)
- *The Psychology of Selling: Increase Your Sales Faster and Easier than You Thought Possible* by Brian Tracy (Thomas Nelson, 2013)
- *The Customer Rules: The 39 Essential Rules for Delivering Sensational Service* by Lee Cockrell (Crown Business, 2005)
- *Uplifting Service: The Proven Path to Delighting Your Customers, Colleagues, and Everyone Else You Meet* by Ron Kaufman (Evolve Publishing, 2012)
- *The Greatest Salesman in the World* by Og Mandino (Bantam, 1983)

If you are looking for a way of making your in-person sessions memorable without relying on technology, a "reveal wall" might be the answer. I first read about this idea for a lightbox-like wall in Sue Bryce's blog post "The Reveal Wall," and I love the method for creating a high-end, luxury experience sans technology. You can find her post at www.inbedwithsue.com/2013/09/06/the-reveal-wall.

Also, Tamara Lackey's Sales, Sales, Sales e-course from CreativeLive is a fantastic resource for gaining a perspective on how others in the industry do in-person sales. For more information, see www.creativelive.com/courses/sales-sales-sales-tamara-lackey.

Writing effective website copy can be a challenge, but it is essential to draw in and hook your ideal client. Here are three of my favorite sources for help and inspiration:

- *Words that Sell: More than 6000 Entries to Help You Promote Your Products, Services and Ideas* by Richard Bayan (McGraw-Hill, 2006)

- *Writing Copy for Dummies* by Johnathan Kranz (For Dummies, 2004)
- "The 10 Essential Ingredients of Successful Sales Pages" by Dave Navarro (Copyblogger, www.copyblogger.com/successful-sales-pages)

Chapter 5 additional resources

Networking and forming co-marketing relationships with other business can be just the boost your business needs. Unfortunately and even unintentionally, those same relationships can also become a legal minefield.

Having key terms of your agreement clarified in writing can help, and I always recommend you hire a lawyer if you want to make sure that you truly are protected by a document. Just because something is in writing doesn't mean that it will hold up in court or that it has the power to protect you. To get you started, I've included a few links to sample contracts to help you draft your ideas, but I encourage you to still seek out legal guidance once you have your framework created to make sure that it fits the needs of your business.

If you need help with wedding contracts or simply legal contracts in general, these sites can help you:

- http://wedding-photographers-directory.com/ContractPDFs/Contract%204.pdf
- www.idophotonet.com/pdf/sample_contract.pdf
- www.designaglow.com/products/complete-legal-wedding-contract

Networking is an excellent way to build relationships that can evolve into fruitful mini-session collaboration. One source to build connections in your community is to network with other entrepreneurs through organizations like BNI (www.bni.com) and Toastmasters (www.toastmasters.com) that may have access to your ideal clients or may actually be your ideal clients. In addition, these are a few excellent books (and some of my favorites) that you should add to your networking library:

- *Little Black Book of Connections: 6.5 Assets for Networking Your Way to Rich Relationships* by Jeffrey Gitomer (Bard Press, 2006)
- *How to Win Friends and Influence People* by Dale Carnegie (Pocket Books, 1998)
- *Networking Is Not Working: Stop Collecting Business Cards and Start Making Meaningful Connections* by Derek Coburn (Ideapress Publishing, 2014)

MARKET LESS, GET PAID MORE WITH A NICHE THAT FITS

> "So, what do you do?"
>
> "Oh, I'm a photographer."
>
> "Really? That's so neat. My niece is a photographer!"
>
> "No kidding? What type of photography does she do?"
>
> "I'm not sure, but she's taking pictures with her phone all the time and posting them on Instagram. She photographs a little bit of everything. My cousin is a photographer, too. He used to do weddings, but now he just does those little pictures for the elementary soccer and T-ball teams. "

Sound familiar?

We've all experienced a version this conversation at least once, gritting our teeth at the end to keep from responding, "Yeah, but I'm a *real* photographer, the kind that gets clients and makes money.

The minute you say that you are a photographer, people will tell you who they know who is also a photographer and start talking all about what that *other person* does. Frustrating, right? Yes, but it doesn't have to be.

When you present yourself as a niche photographer, the conversation can go very differently.

"So, what do you do?"

"Oh, I'm a branding and image photographer for entrepreneurial women."

"Really? Wow, I've never heard of that before! So, what do you actually do with that?"

"Well, I work with women who have small businesses with online presences. I provide photography for their websites and marketing materials that authentically depict their identity and communicates their branding message in a visual way. It helps them attract better clients and build trust by having a more authentic and professional web appearance.

"What's your website? I have a friend who has a new business that so needs this! Do you have a card or something? I want to tell her about you! "

See how that works? Suddenly, you're not just another photographer; you're in the business of helping people.

Find your niche

When you present yourself as a commodity, people don't think about you; they think about someone they know who does the same thing as they *think* you do. They don't see you as someone who helps people with needs, needs that they or someone they know might have. Opening a conversation where someone can talk to you about their interests is not a bad thing, if you are building relationships. If you are marketing, however, you just lost a potential word-of-mouth marketer or a potential client. You missed an opportunity to help someone.

But when you have a specialization, a *niche*, the thing that you do instantly becomes what others want to talk about. You are more than just a photographer; you are a person who *helps* people do better things, and you are an expert. People want to know more about what you do, and, most importantly, they begin to think of their own needs or the needs of someone they might know who can use you. You've just planted a marketing seed.

Your target market is not your niche. Your photography is not your niche. Your niche is a combination of three things that put you into a smaller category of specialization:

- The people you serve
- The problems you help solve
- Your signature method of producing and serving

When you clearly define and establish these three areas, you have your niche. When you specialize in a niche, you are opening up yourself to more opportunities by eliminating the reputation that comes along with being "a photographer," which is basically that you use a camera and may or may not make money at it. Being just "a photographer" is limiting, and it doesn't reveal what you do. Even saying you are a wedding photographer or a senior photographer is still limiting, as not every client wants the same type of wedding or senior photographer. Defining your niche also helps you shift the way you internally perceive your business and your clients, and how you serve them, so that you can further brainstorm ideas about what you are doing within your niche to best serve it.

Plant a marketing seed

Most nonphotographers don't even realize how much a photographer can serve them until the inspiration is planted in their minds. Although an entrepreneur may know he needs an image of his smiling face on his website, for example, he may not realize how much the right photographer can help him. Together, you can create images that better fit his branding and create a visual bridge to his marketing message, a bridge that helps him fix the problems he has been having with his website images.

For a marketing seed to take root, it needs to resonate with the struggles and frustrations potential clients are experiencing and to explain how you are the solution. For example, you need to first point out to the entrepreneur that you understand his struggle, link it to not having the right images on his website, and point out the side effects it may be having on his business. He may not have realized a lack of quality images can lead to a lack of trust within the marketplace, for instance, or that the right social media images could vastly strengthen his online presence. Once the entrepreneur can see these needs, he can then see the bigger picture of how images have an impact on improving his marketing message and business overall. Then he can see it's bigger than hiring a photographer to update a headshot.

Expertise worth paying for

Specializing makes your business personal, and even more importantly, it makes you a stand out as an expert on the subject. You become *the* go-to person. Instead of being chosen (or being overlooked) because of your pricing, you are chosen for your expertise.

Everyone knows, experts get paid more. The highly trained technician at the Audi dealership commands a better rate than the general mechanic at the In-N-Out garage. Some people will be willing to part with more money in exchange for being able to have the expert, while others won't value the expert at all and will go for what is cheapest. You want to seek out the people who are looking for the expert.

When people understand how you can help them, decide you're offering something that they truly want, and are willing to pay for, that's what leads to more sales, higher fees, and being sought after. The more specialized that you are, the more people you can help!

Solving problems, serving needs

When you specialize in your niche, you don't have to fight for a piece of the pie. You actually make the pie bigger. When I found my niche as a photographer of newborn babies (see the sidebar "Hitting Upon My Niche"), I wasn't taking clients away from another photographer as my bookings grew because I was able to serve clients who weren't being served. The type of clients who were hiring me couldn't previously find the right fit for their needs, so instead, they went without and didn't hire any photographer.

By choosing a niche that fit my needs and the needs of my clients, I was able to have a profitable and sustainable business model. Bringing in ideal clients required little marketing because of how I stood out in the community with my niche; I was seen as an expert, which drew my clients to me like magnets. My business met all three criteria that define a magnetic niche:

- **Serve a specific group.** My clients were very specific. They wanted images of their newborn baby during that window of time when their bitty one actually looks bitty, sleepy, fresh, and new.
- **Solve their problems.** Most studios wouldn't photograph newborns until they were six weeks old or sometimes even older. Those that did would capture these weird, posed images using awkward props, usually while baby was awake. Awake newborn pictures are generally awkward

because the babies throw out their arms and legs and have that adorable, but nonphotogenic cross-eyed stare.

- **Serve their needs in a unique way.** Because I had a low-volume studio model, I was able to book only one session per day, which gave me the opportunity to dedicate several hours to one client without the pressure of working around others. The amount of time I spent with each client built trust that I was going to make sure that their needs were met. A lot of new parents were worried about the investment because they were unsure how their little one would "perform." I was able to assure them that we would give baby all the time that she needed.

Keep track of the relevant problems that your clients are having while working with other photographers, and keep adding those solutions to your niche business. For instance, I found all other photographers had a two-week or longer turnaround, so I offered a five-day turnaround so clients could get their newborn announcements out right away. Coming back to the studio to do the ordering session was often a struggle for new parents, so I began offering online ordering or home visits to help them order. For clients unable to come in to my studio at all, I arranged in-home sessions.

The more you listen to the needs of your ideal client and look for solutions to those problems, the more refined your niche will become. My business turned into serving my niche instead of selling my art. Although art was still the end result, clients were drawn to me mostly because they knew I would take care of their needs. Other photographers were just as good or better than me, but I was the one clients chose because I had built that trust factor; I was the best choice to take care of the things that mattered the most to them.

When you choose a niche, you can stop chasing after business and instead allow business to flow in to you. The more you grow in your niche, you reach a magical tipping point where you will barely even need to market to get all the clients you need. Consider the case of a photographer who I coach. In 2013 she was on the brink of closing her Washington, DC, studio. After we worked on a few changes to refine her niche, she began to see a huge change in the flow of clients. In a few months, she went from feeling desperate to get another client to further refining her niche to eliminate *extra* clients that were no longer a good fit for her business because her calendar was filling up so rapidly with her ideal clients. Once she began to serve the ideal client only, word-of-mouth marketing began to magnetically pull in more clients like the ones she was serving.

HITTING UPON MY NICHE

When I first started my photography business, I knew nothing about specializing, niches, or micro niches. I did know I was exhausted and discontent with taking every client who came my way. True, I needed to make money, but more importantly, I wanted to make money while enjoying my work.

While I was shooting anything and everything, I started paying attention to what was making the most money, so I could then expand on doing just that and eliminate what wasn't paying me as well. Quickly, I learned babies made bucks. Doing newborn work in my natural-light studio space was my best seller.

At the time, my competition photographed everything from weddings to babies to commercial jobs. I was the only exclusive baby photographer, which immediately made me stand out. I also was the only one with a natural-light studio space and the only one who worked with newborns from three days old.

Because I chose to have a high-sale, low-volume model for my studio, I could take one client per day, which allowed me to take newborns when most other studios were turning them away because they couldn't dedicate three to four hours to a session. I found my niche, and it paid me very well.

No longer was I just another photographer in the community; I was *The* Newborn Photographer, an expert and specialist. The word-of-mouth marketing spread was magical; I was finding the perfect clients who wanted what I offered because no one else was offering it in the same way.

At the time, I had four little ones of my own, so I related to a lot of my clients and understood their needs. I tailored the way that I served them to meet those needs before they even had to ask. Brand new babies were welcome; no need to wait until six weeks. My clients were drawn to the fact that I offered no-pressure, relaxed sessions; some took two hours, some took four. I did whatever necessary to get the very best images for the clients. I also let the slightly frazzled and sleep-deprived parents know that I even had a couch in the studio that was perfect for a nap, if needed.

I loved this type of work not only because it paid me well but also because my clients valued me and appreciated what I offered and how I served their needs. My clients would then refer their pregnant friends to me, and the word-of-mouth marketing spread like wildfire.

I transformed from being the new photographer in town to being *The* Newborn Photographer in less than a year because of one simple fact: I built my business around a niche. I wasn't competing with the other photographers in the marketplace; I carved out my own little marketplace.

Keep your niche authentic

Do you hate marketing because you feel like a sleazy car salesman desperate for business? If so, that's a screaming warning that you are approaching your business as a commodity instead of a solution to a problem. With a niche that feels authentic to you, the leads come to you instead of you having to chase after business, convincing everyone you come in contact with that you are the photographer they need. Marketing begins to feel effortless because you talk about your business in a way that lights you up.

When you are using the best of your abilities doing what you are passionate about and confident in, you market effortlessly. It doesn't feel like a burden or unnatural. The unnatural feeling comes from when you are trying to sell something that you don't believe in, especially if you are selling yourself as a commodity instead of selling yourself as a problem solver. Doctors don't squirm at their pricing. They aren't seen as commodities; they are seen as problem solvers.

Once you are marketing within your niche, you will begin to hear fewer generic inquiries ("I need a photographer. Can you send me your pricelist?") and more requests like "I've heard amazing things about you. I understand that you are the perfect person to help me with *[the person's needs]*. Tell me how I can work with you."

A lot of business gurus teach that you need to pick a niche that pays the most and then stay there. But for most in creative work, the money isn't the strongest motivator, so choosing a niche based on what pays best feels just as inauthentic as being a commodity. Money matters little when your heart is not into all that you are doing in your business. If your heart is not in what you are doing, you can't love the people you serve. If you can't love the people you serve, your motivation to grow the quality of your business will be nonexistent because you can't connect emotionally and you won't see clients as people with needs that you can solve.

When your heart is not into your business, you will find that the money and clients will slowly (or maybe even rapidly) dwindle because you will subconsciously be pushing away business by not looking for the best clients or putting out your best marketing efforts. You'll find yourself back in survival mode instead of investing in growth. What may seem like a well-paying niche can actually turn into a starving one when it's not the one for you.

THE FEAR OF LEAVING CLIENTS BEHIND

Choosing a niche initially can feel like being exclusive instead of inclusive. You may feel more inauthentic by having to choose a niche because you feel like you are leaving out a large group of people. Especially for women, it goes against our nature to cut off or eliminate people.

Specializing actually *does* leave people out, but you are leaving out the people who don't get you, don't really resonate with what you do, and who skip hiring you because they don't understand who you are or what you do. If you are currently struggling to get hired, you are already experiencing this loss. People come in contact with your business but skip hiring you because they don't understand what it is that you do and how you can help them. You already are leaving these people out, but you aren't leaving them out on your terms.

With specializing, you can leave out people on *your* terms, which is a much healthier place. Leave out the people who don't resonate with what you offer, and embrace the people who do. The more people who understand you, the more people who will hire you. By becoming more understandable, you are widening your marketplace.

When you shift into a niche that feels authentic and exciting to you because you love the people, love solving their problems, and love the methods in which you do it all, then that's the perfect niche for you and the one that is going to pay you handsomely.

Expand your opportunities, define your niche

note If you currently aren't specializing in a niche (or you have no desire to), your lack of specialization doesn't make you less of entrepreneur or imply that you have a shortcoming in your dedication to your business. A lack of specialization merely is a gap in opportunity.

To be a strong entrepreneur, you don't have to change into someone you aren't; simply choose to do only what you do best and eliminate all the rest. By choosing a niche, you can then eliminate the distractions of everything that you *could* be doing and instead focus on one thing. By eliminating all the overwhelming options and mental clutter, you can to stretch your creativity further to experiment more within that chosen niche instead of bouncing around like a rubber ball.

When you start expanding your creativity within your niche, you take fewer risks but are more of an innovator within that niche. You can be a tad bit outrageous and try new things. If they don't work, then it's a lesson learned that can help you further refine your strengths and eliminate what isn't working.

As when changing your pricing, be decisive about choosing your niche. Yes, it can be somewhat scary because you feel like you're cutting off your plan B.

What happens if this niche doesn't work or you don't like it? Are you committed forever? Remember, however, that it's uncomfortable only because it is new and unfamiliar. Once you see the benefits, you'll find yourself embracing your niche even more readily because of how it serves you. You either will have a lucrative, viable niche or you won't. Being indecisive is going to keep you stuck forever. It's better to choose wrong than not to choose at all. The best part about being self-employed is it's your prerogative to change your mind. If something isn't working, you can always change.

Niche worksheets

So, you've decided being a niche photographer is the best move for your business, and maybe you even have a loose idea of what your niche is. That's a start, but as when you defined your ideal client, you need to delve deeper. In fact, thinking of the clients, or even ideal clients, *within* your niche is the best way. The "People I Serve and Problems I Can Solve" worksheet will help you refine your thoughts.

It may take you awhile to really nail down your answers, so don't feel the need to rush it. Just lean into the process of thinking through this person and his or her problems and emotions so that you can begin to find a way that you uniquely can solve the person's problems. Brain dump and write down as many ideas and thoughts as you can and then narrow down to the ones that resonate the most strongly with you.

Defining your niche is a journey as well. It may take several rounds of going through this process before you arrive at that magical combination. Experience will be your best teacher as you further laser in on your niche, allowing you to fine-tune it more and more as your business develops.

Don't feel like you have to get it perfect before you can take a step forward. Each step that you take in refining your niche is progress, but only if you actually follow through with taking that step; don't leave it rattling around in your idea box.

Once you complete the "People I Serve and Problems I Can Solve" worksheet, you can summarize what you are in the business of doing by going through the "I Am in the Business of Helping" worksheet. Each time you complete the "I am in the business of" prompt, refine your thoughts until you have put together a magical combination that gives your specialized niche a definition. (Don't limit yourself to the number of repetitions listed in the worksheet. In a book, my space is limited, but you can keep refining for as many pages as you need.)

PEOPLE I SERVE AND PROBLEMS I CAN SOLVE

The type of people in my niche are *(ask yourself, "Who are they, and what do they want?")*:

Problems that they experience getting what they want are:

Emotions these problems cause them to feel are:

Solutions they want to their experience are *(think of behavior or specific situations in describing this)*:

What they really want is...

I AM IN THE BUSINESS OF HELPING

Start with the basics:

I'm not a photographer anymore. I'm in the business of helping

____ (people)
with ____ (problem)
by ____ (the things I do).

Refine your message:

Examples:

I am in the business of photographing the last days of a beloved pet for its owners and providing a final memento to celebrate the life and memories of that pet before it passes.

I am in the business of artistic storytelling photography for eclectic brides who aren't satisfied with status quo images to remember their memorable wedding day.

I am in the business of...

____

____

____

____

I am in the business of...

____

____

____

____

I am in the business of...

____

____

____

____

I am in the business of...

____

____

____

____

Your signature system

Your niche differentiates you from the competition, as does the way you serve clients in that niche. So far, we've focused on the defining the niche itself; now you need to examine the way you serve it. You need to work on your *signature system*, the series of steps that takes your clients through your client workflow from beginning to the end and gets the results they want. A client workflow is more than just an organizational system to get your client from one end of the experience with you to the other. It differentiates you from all the other photographers. While using someone else's workflow can be a great starting point, implementing it exactly step by step takes *you* out of the way you serve. You're serving someone else's way. When you specialize, your workflow, the rhythm and order that you take your clients through, must be unique.

Create a signature system

When evolving your signature system, start with what you know. Don't try to sell something that you aren't yet comfortable with and don't feel confident in. Give your ideas time to develop so that you can present yourself as an expert. It may take using some clients as test subjects and practicing on them, which is an excellent way to get comfortable with what you are doing within your niche. Don't be afraid to practice, but don't practice on paying clients if you are presenting yourself as an expert.

You don't need to be an organizational guru to be able to create your own client workflow system. The pieces to your system will be easy to put together and systemize when you look at your clients (who you love!) and the problems they have. A signature system won't work if it's a cookie-cutter solution; it needs to be what works best for *you* and what you can maintain. If it feels overly complicated, then it's most likely because you are trying to do something that doesn't fit you *or* your clients' needs in the best way. Focus on their needs, and make sure every step of the process serves them. Do what you do best while addressing those needs. The questions that you need to ask yourself to define your signature system are listed in the "Your Niche Signature System" worksheet.

Your niche signature system example

How might you fill out the "Niche Signature System" worksheet? The sample answers that follow are for a micro-niche-based photographer who focuses on branding and image photography for entrepreneurial women. Call her business the Entrepreneurial Woman Photographer.

Don't wait to begin the process

Please remember, your signature system is more than a process that you take your clients through. It is a process that you will take yourself through to continually find ways to differentiate yourself from your competition.

As you take your client through your system, use it as a process to get to know and understand your clients better. In the beginning stages, it will be a way to refine who you are and what you do for them while giving amazing value and service throughout the entire experience of working with you. But most importantly, it will help you to stay on top of problem areas to find simple and easily implemented solutions that you can keep repeating over and over to build a solid brand experience, which in time will help your business run like clockwork.

Don't wait to begin implementing your signature system until you have all the pieces put together. If all the pieces are overwhelming, start with one thing. Just get started. Putting it off for the sake of perfection is going to slow down your progress to becoming the expert in your niche—and you could potentially lose clients to someone else who is hungrier than you to have their business!

note If you want a lifelong love affair with your business by focusing on a specialization that positions you as the expert and authority in your marketplace and industry, visit me at www.profitfirstphotography.com. I will teach you to stand out in your marketplace in how you serve clients who are obsessed with you and what you do.

YOUR NICHE SIGNATURE SYSTEM

What do I want my clients to know before they contact me?

What do I want my clients to have or know once they contact me?

What do I give my clients after initial inquiry?

What process do I take my clients through in the pre-hiring consult?

continues on next page

YOUR NICHE SIGNATURE SYSTEM (continued)

What are the steps that I take my clients through from the time they book to the time of the photoshoot?

What happens after the session?

What happens between the ordering session and the delivery?

What happens after delivery?

How do I follow up?

How do I stay in contact?

YOUR NICHE SIGNATURE SYSTEM (EXAMPLE)

What do I want my clients to know before they contact me?

#1: Free e-mail list opt-in: 5 ways to use photography to improve your marketing. (Hook piece for entrepreneur women to give them 5 examples of how photography can be used beyond a headshot on the website to inspire them to consider having a session for more than just a headshot.) Includes information about booking their own session with the Entrepreneurial Woman Photographer and introduces them to the process of working with her.

#2: Website copy: Work-with-me page describes signature system in step-by-step detail of what to expect including features and benefits.

#3: E-mail inquiry form questionnaire; along with name and contact details, include these questions in the form:

What is your biggest frustration currently with your website and images?

Do you struggle to know how to put your brand and marketing message more into your visual appearance online?

Are you currently satisfied with your visual identity online? What feels the most "off" to you?

What do I want my clients to have or know once they contact me?

E-mail inquiry auto-responder: bonus PDF, how to attract better clients with your visual branding (another hook piece educating the client on the various ways that having branded imagery will improve their marketing and overall business)

What do I give my clients after initial inquiry?

Schedule one-on-one call with client to do a pre-booking conversion conversation; questionnaire that asks what are your greatest needs and biggest struggles with your personal branding image?

Convert client to session:

Type #1: "I have my brand" for clients who have their branding established and are ready for the photoshoot. Includes marketing calendar planner for clients to use with their social media images.

Type #2: For clients who need more intensive coaching before their sessions to determine marketing message, colors, style, and how to bring it all together.

Type #3: For clients who need done-for-you service from outfit planning, stylist, and one-on-one coaching and planning the photoshoot. Bonus marketing calendar planner for social media images planning.

What process do I take my clients through in the pre-hiring consult?

Signature Session Planner

Step 1: Your marketing message

Step 2: Your personality

Step 3: Your style

Step 4: Your colors

Step 5: Bringing it altogether

Bonus: Bonus PDF to favorite vendors (web designer, website coder, virtual assistant, editor, social media manager, etc.)

(Session type 1, DIY worksheet; session type 2, one consult call/in-person meeting working on the worksheet together; session type 3: three 2-hour in-person coaching sessions)

Step 6: Session planner/approval

Step 7: Location confirmation and team setup (stylist, makeup artist, assistant, etc.)

continues on next page

YOUR NICHE SIGNATURE SYSTEM (EXAMPLE) (continued)

What are the steps that I take my clients through from the time they book to the time of the photoshoot?

Pre-session consult(s)
E-mail and text reminder week before session (getting ready for your session details)
E-mail and text reminder day before session (final arrangement of details)
Phone call day of session confirming (are you excited or what!?)

What happens after the session?

Instagram single-image sneak peek
Social media teaser trailer video (30-second video behind the scenes from the session) and mini-testimonial from client of how she felt during the session and why she hired the Entrepreneurial Woman Photographer

What happens between the ordering session and the delivery?

Delivery of digital images (online upload for client download)
Blog post interview/business feature with sneek peek of images (blog posting date determined by client depending on website image launch)
Newsletter feature promoting client's business
Add client to "Inner Circle" Facebook group for clients to share business information and have access to a community support system for networking

What happens after delivery?

Mail thank-you card and flower arrangement

How do I follow up?

6 months after image delivery, do follow-up consult to find out how the images are working for the client's website (what's working/what's not) and to see if the client needs more filler images for the marketing calendar

How do I stay in contact?

VIP client special newsletter once per month with special promos, discounts, business tip of the month, vendor feature, etc.

Follow their social media pages and check in once a month to comment on their work/posts and promote

INDEX

R

S

Y